PRAISE FOR

slightly above average

"We should all be so lucky to live in a village that has Sandi Marx as its idiot. This funny, spunky, extraordinary lady has the STORIES—gather 'round and enjoy!"

EMILY FLAKE, owner and operator of St. Nell's Humor Writing Residency and writer and cartoonist for *New Yorker* magazine

"At the beginning of Sandi Marx's new memoir, she writes that she's somehow slid by with no 'strong life skills or talent.' But these hilarious, clever, and at times heartbreaking stories show that she has both—in droves."

DAVID CRABB, author of *Bad Kid: A Memoir* and member of The Groundlings

"When Sandi Marx is sharing a story, I buckle up for a helluva ride! She's just the most fabulously funny observer of this absurd catastrophe we call life."

KEVIN ALLISON, bestselling author, comedian, performing member of The State, and host of RISK!

"What a joy to dive into Sandi Marx's hilarious adventures! Her eye for comic detail and delicious prose style are a tonic. If you need a mood boost, skip the caffeine and reach for this book. I didn't want it to end!"

BARBARA FELDON, actor and author of *Getting Smarter*

slightly above average

slightly above average

MEMOIRS OF A ~~SUCCESSFUL~~ VILLAGE IDIOT

sandi marx

Published by

**MANDALA
TREE** PRESS
mandalatreepress.com

Paperback ISBN: 9781954801776
Hardcover with Dust Jacket ISBN: 9781954801783
Case Laminate ISBN: 9781954801790
eBook ISBN: 9781954801806

HUMOo3000 Humor/Essays
PERO19000 performing arts/storytelling
BIO026000 bio/ personal memoir

Cover design and typesetting by Kaitlin Barwick
Edited by Deborah Spencer and Valene Wood

sandijmarx.com

FOR RHONDA

CONTENTS

CONTENTS

Author's Note

All of these essays are as accurate as my memory will allow. In other words, if you fact check, you might find a few minor errors like timelines, geography, and other details. A few names have been changed to protect the guilty. But the events described are true nonetheless.

These are my stories.

INTRODUCTION

I JUMP OUT OF MY UBER ON TWENTY-THIRD Street in Chelsea, hoping to get to the movie theater on time. I struggle to get over the curb with my broken foot in an unwieldy plastic cast. I also need the driver to remove my foot trolley out of his trunk. He's not thrilled with having to wrestle a walking device that neither one of us could figure out how to fold or collapse.

It's been a couple of weeks since my car accident and somehow I still can't stop myself from telling every Uber driver how one of their colleagues mowed me down on Franklin Ave. in Brooklyn. Am I subconsciously sending a message, "You better watch for pedestrians!" or am I just that inappropriate idiot who can't run my thoughts through a filter before I speak? I suppose I'm a little bit of both and frankly, it still stuns me that at sixty-six years of age, I haven't faced any serious consequences for some of my actions.

I manage to roll myself inside the Cineplex and at that moment it hits me; I am here for the premiere of a documentary that is all about *me*! I have been able to pull the proverbial wool over everyone's eyes my whole life, and somehow it's culminated into a director choosing to spend three years of his professional life following me around and documenting—well, pretty much everything. This little film managed to find its way from the Big Apple Film Festival to Cannes and win a bunch of awards along the way, and now resides on Amazon Prime Video.

Why?

Who knows? I swear, I'm not that interesting, and I am not exactly a prophet. I'm more like the protagonist in the film *Being There*. I'm not a gardener, but I seem to be very good at spreading some serious bullshit. This book of essays will illustrate how I managed, in all my perceived mediocrity, to have a fulfilling and wildly adventurous life without any strong life skills or talent.

I can honestly say it all began when my fourth-grade teacher wrote on my report card that in spite of my troubling grades, I played well with others. I was considered cooperative—which apparently, when you are nine, is an asset. Looking back, it makes me think I slid by in every school year because I was a skilled ass kisser.

We've all heard about EQ versus IQ. I am here to report that being really smart is not always as effective as understanding how to read a room. Even as a kid, I had figured out how to get adults on my side. I know it's because my parents were always deeply concerned about our financial woes and my older sister, who was constantly sick. Humor and a distracting compliment can win the day.

Obviously, this trickery wasn't as potent by the time I got to college, but God knows I tried. The very idea that I was accepted to a legit school with my 750 *combined* score on my SATs is a feat in itself. Not only was I accepted to the University of South Florida, I got a full scholarship. The year I applied coincided with the same year that particular school started a theater program and really wanted students from New York. Maybe they thought that, in a city famous for the expression, "If you can make it here, you can make it anywhere," New York aspiring actors must be good. I certainly wasn't going to disavow that notion. Instead, like so many times in my life, I leaned in for the free ride.

In spite of family tragedies and challenges I've faced my whole life, somehow there has been a balancing of cosmic scales that has led me to this moment, stepping and repeating for local press, at the Big Apple Film Festival with Frank Ruy, my talented director. With our lanyards and badges, we walk (I roll) down a red carpet and inside the screening of *The Fabulist*. I have a feeling that Frank, in his cheeky way, named the movie *The Fabulist* so audiences could decide if everything they were watching was a story about a woman who is either a lauded storyteller or maybe someone with a knack for making up fantastical fables.

As in most of my "larger than an average" middle-aged woman's life, this film happened because Frank watched me perform at a story-telling event at the work space called The Yard. He approached me that night and excitedly started to ask if I'd be interested in being a subject of a film chronicling my life. Why? I knew he wasn't the guy who wanted to get me in a closet, tie me up with bungee cords, and film me trying to escape. He had sent me examples of his work and he was legit and earnest. Would Frank figure out what I already knew about myself? That I am not particularly interesting nor is there enough material for a full-length film?

Since I haven't "buried the lede," you already know that, in spite of my self-flagellation and lack of self-respect, apparently I am more interesting than I might have initially thought.

This book is a series of stories that will show you how a soupçon of ineptitude, mixed results in a scholastic career and a willingness to expose my flaws can still lead to a successful and fulfilling life. It's called a memoir, even if that sounds a bit lofty, because I do not really think of myself as anything more than slightly above average, and a lot of my good fortune has happened because of luck and timing and the one singularly important life skill: a good sense of humor. As you will read, I have managed to climb out of not one but two major earthquakes, to accidentally mug a teenager, to survive white water rafting, to avoid a near miss with a con man, to experience a robbery in progress, to survive a fateful car accident, and so much more.

I do not claim to be qualified to offer the kind of life skills that are necessarily useful to you, but, hey, who knows? Being slightly above average just might be the ticket to a well-lived life.

Over the Rainbow

HOT LAVA! HOT LAVA! HOW MANY OF US CAN conjure childhood memories when we hear those two words? It was the equivalent of Marco Polo, without a chlorinated swimming pool. My sister, Rhonda (three years my elder), and I spent countless hours in our tiny, below-street-level bedroom jumping from one of our twin beds to the other shouting those words. God forbid we jump and fall on our high pile, green shag, wall-to-wall carpeting—in our imagination, skin grafts would be in order.

At first glance, our room looked pretty much like any other pre-adolescent childhood bedroom, but it was quite different on closer inspection. Next to the shelves stacked with Monopoly, Mystery

Date, and our Barbie Dreamhouse, there were rows of exotic sounding medications like Digitalis and boxes of gauze pads stacked high. A brown stain had formed where a bottle of Peroxide sat because the cap was never properly put back. All in all, this wall of toxicity prevention resembled a triage unit at any local emergency room.

By the time I was twelve, I had become my sister's keeper. If she forgot to take her medicine or had a suspicious cough, it was my job to narc on her. This was not a job I applied for, nor did I expect to also be asked to be the one in our family to act as a stool pigeon. Let me explain. When Rhonda was born in 1953, neonatal care and preventative medicine was, you can pardon the pun, in its infancy. My sister had a hole in her heart. The doctor told my parents after Rhonda was born that her life expectancy was about five years. Devastating information and thankfully inaccurate. Unfortunately, she did need multiple surgeries and grueling tests, like a heart catheterization, which in the mid-1960s was a torturous affair, requiring her to lay still for seven hours while long needles and tubes were inserted in her wrists and groin. She could barely hold a pen for a year after that debacle.

What made this indignation even worse was the fact that Rhonda's passions were painting and sewing and she could do neither while recuperating. In spite of her situation, she never complained. I suppose if you are born with challenges and chronic illness, you don't know what you are missing. But I knew and was hyper aware that any strenuous activity on my part could make her feel jealous.

This was completely self-imposed. I suppose my mother, Greta, stoked this particular fire by restricting a lot of my hobbies by claiming they were too dangerous. Our favorite pastime usually involved watching endless television. In those days the options were limited to four channels: CBS, ABC, NBC, and PBS. There was zero chance we would watch PBS and accidentally learn something. We loved shows like *I Dream of Jeannie*. We'd stand up and follow Barbara Eden (the star of the show), cross our arms and blink, praying that just like Jeannie, we could disappear from this room and be somewhere exotic. Our black-and-white TV had tin foil on the antenna for HD quality, and, because it wasn't operated by remote control, we had to get up to change the channel—oh, and the dial got "lost" somehow and we used pliers to switch channels.

This was our survival, because the shouting going on in our dinette between our parents was so loud and terrifying, we figured if we just turned up the volume on *My Mother the Car*, maybe it wasn't really happening? As a side note, I still use this methodology while walking the noisy streets of New York with my headphones blasting my favorite crime podcasts.

In addition to the screaming matches, always about money, our apartment was incredibly hot. There was a large steam pipe in our front hall that I still maintain heated the entire F line in our building. We had no air conditioning in the summer, just floor fans that could take a finger with just one glance and windows that barely opened because of the sloppy old paint job. Because of the sweat box atmosphere, Greta wore as little as possible. A buxom gal, she usually donned her brassiere, the kind that had about thirty eyes and hooks, and her large lady underpants. Arnold, my dad, wore a white tee shirt and his boxers. That tee always had unidentifiable stains, which even at a young age, I thought seemed grossly inappropriate.

My mom was not a cook. She even owned and utilized a cookbook called *The I Hate to Cook Book* by a funny lady named Peg Bracken. Her favorite recipes usually involved a Campbell's soup like cream of mushroom, which would get slathered on pork chops, or her personal favorite, vegetable soup with alphabet noodles mixed in her meatloaf. There is nothing as unappealing as sitting at a kitchen table, parents yelling at each other between bites, and watching food flying from their mouths. Greta, in that bra, with alphabet letters sitting in her sweaty continental shelf (or as you would call it, her cleavage). Rhonda and I would beg to eat in our room and our mom usually acquiesced.

The best time of the year was when *The Wizard of Oz* came on television. Fun fact, we had our minds blown when we finally got a portable color television and realized the Emerald City was so colorful. We made our mom bake us our favorite

Swanson TV dinners, the one with turkey breast and a peach cobbler, and sit, transfixed at our snack tables enjoying a movie we could practically recite. When Dorothy would click her heels and say, "There's no place like home," we'd be clicking our heels and saying, "Can we please leave home?"

When the weather was warm, we were allowed to play on our street, Yellowstone Blvd. We owned one pair of roller skates, but we did not take turns rolling down the block, that would be way too strenuous for Rhonda. So we perfected the art of the roll walk. I'd wear the right, she, the left, and, while holding hands, we'd walk/roll to the corner. Sometimes we'd walk to our local playground, just two blocks away and hang out on the swings.

Because Rhonda had terrible circulation, her lips were purple and kids liked to tease her. I was not having it and I'd get up in these bullies' grill and threaten to knock them out. I might add here, at twelve years old, I was about fifty pounds and maybe four feet tall. Hell hath no fury like a sister's keeper. Rhonda went to a different junior and senior high school than I did because back then, there weren't necessarily accommodations for students with special needs. All she needed was an elevator, but because Forest Hills High didn't have one, every day a short bus picked her up and took her to Francis Lewis High, a twenty-minute drive away.

All of her school chums had different disabilities. There was Rachel, who was her best friend and blind, and her boyfriend Jerry, who was wheelchair bound with cerebral palsy. I found her friends fascinating and loved when that bus dropped Rhonda and her classmates at our apartment for playdates, which back then were *not* referred to as such, just hang outs. I used to fantasize that I was an emcee like Jerry Lewis hosting a telethon, offering refreshments to Rhonda's friends while watching them scuff my mom's walls with their wheelchairs. The more the merrier was my hope for these impromptu parties.

Rhonda was still defying the odds at twenty-one years old. A college student, engaged to marry Jerry and living on campus, she was thriving. I was no longer spending my nights listening for her congested coughs or monitoring her pharmaceutical intake, I was just obliviously living my teenage life—until the inevitable became our reality.

On a hot July morning, Rhonda felt exhausted and unwell. I had just left for a summer in the Catskills as a camp counselor and didn't give much thought as to why Rhonda didn't wake up to say goodbye. Three days later, I was called into the head counselor's office and was told to pack a bag because my parents were picking me up. At this point, my mind went into denial overdrive and assumed Rhonda was in the hospital and wanted my company. I was wrong. As soon as my mom's Ford Pinto pulled up the gravel driveway, one look at her face and I knew. Rhonda, my brilliant, beautiful sister, my first real love, was gone. I climbed in the back seat and numbly asked what I already knew and didn't want to hear. I am still grieving the loss, almost fifty years later. I wouldn't get to be her gatekeeper ever again.

I still watch *The Wizard of Oz* on occasion, usually with my kids, and when I see Dorothy clicking her heels, I now think there *is* no place like my childhood home. I wish I could be back in that cluttered bedroom with the shag carpeting, holding Rhonda's hand and dreaming of our life together in a couple of pairs of ruby slippers.

Hebrew School Dropout

RHONDA AND I WERE STANDING IN FRONT OF Temple Sinai. We had just gotten out of Hebrew school and we *hated* Hebrew school. After an entire year, all I knew was *HaShem Shalee Sandi,* "My name is Sandi." We were clutching our workbooks, waiting for our mom to pick us up and not wanting anyone to see us getting into our family death trap. You could hear her before she made the turn into 112th Street because the muffler on our Dodge Dart was dangling, creating noise and throwing off a few random sparks.

She pulled up, threw open a door, and yelled in a uncharacteristic voice, *"Get in!"* You'd think she just robbed a local Baskin Robbins and wanted us to get home before the ice cream melted. Her face was beet red, and she looked as if smoke could come out of her ears, cartoon style. Obviously, something was up, and before I could ask, she blurted out, "No more Hebrew school! We've been kicked out!"

Rhonda and I looked at each other and smiled. *No more Hebrew school? There is a God, and he's answered our prayers!*

Greta continued. The special fund for families who can't afford the tuition had been depleted. Apparently, Rabbi Shacter went to Israel and brought back the Ten Commandments and used the funds for his trip. I was ten years old and a literal thinker, so I had many follow-up questions. "The rabbi brought back the actual Ten Commandments?"

With her death stare, she snaps, "No, you idiot! Not the actual Ten Commandments! Replicas! To adorn the facade of the temple!"

Ahhhhh. That made sense, even though I still couldn't understand why he had to go all the way to Israel for a fake set of tablets. But frankly, the very notion that the State of Israel would relinquish those historic commandments of literal Biblical proportions to a reformed temple in Queens, New York, did seem implausible.

Unfortunately, being kicked out of Hebrew school was the least of our problems. Sitting on our kitchen table was a stack of unpaid bills that would never get paid. Mostly from doctor offices, labs, and hospitals. The real elephant in the room was my sister Rhonda's tenuous health. In and out of the hospital ever since I could remember, she had that small hole in her heart that couldn't be treated in 1966. With today's technology, the hole could have been closed before she was born, but unfortunately that was just science fiction back then.

My poor parents were dealing with so much all of the time, it's a miracle we ever went to Hebrew school in the first place. From that day on, my family stopped celebrating any of the Jewish holidays that required a temple visit. We were really showing them! Of course, we might not have been observant Jews, but we still loved Passover Seder and Chanukah. The celebration, the stuffed cabbage—that was enough. I never missed a friend's or relative's bar mitzvah, but we didn't really miss having one ourselves either.

Then, the unthinkable but inevitable happened. Rhonda died at twenty-one years old in 1974. The weekend of July 4th, to be precise. Never get sick on a holiday weekend. Her cardiologist was on a golf course, and because it was the first week in July, a whole new rotation of residents and interns were on duty at Long Island Jewish Hospital. With no one there knowing her complicated case, she was doomed.

In our grief, we had to plan her funeral. I was eighteen years old at the time and certainly ill equipped, both emotionally and intellectually, to write my own tribute to honor my only sibling, my first love. The other challenge was the fact that we had not been back to the temple and did not have a family rabbi to counsel us during this horrific time, so we had to outsource. Basically rent a rabbi. In 1974, there wasn't Google or Angie's List; word of mouth was the only solution.

After a bit of crowdsourcing, we went and met with Rabbi Schwartz in his study. I hated him the minute I walked into his cluttered, dark office. Never trust a professional whose desk is covered in old Dunkin' Donuts wrappers. His suit had an unnatural sheen to it (I guess he ironed it), and there were dandruff flakes the size of asbestos chips on his shoulders. He looked like an everything bagel, even sporting an errant poppy seed between his two front teeth. This disheveled dude was going to tell a congregation of our friends and family about our beloved?

It was important to us that he get it right. We sat there and wrote all the things he must say about this brilliant, kind, and beautiful young woman. How she wanted to be a painter, and had managed, in spite of her failing health, to go to college. Rhonda had fallen in love and planned to marry Jerry, her boyfriend. The loving sister and daughter who generously cared for everyone she knew. Her quirky habit of always wearing two different socks and how she sewed her own clothes. Creative and funny, she was pure love. Could this rabbi convey this?

We weren't convinced, but we had no other option. The next morning hundreds of people filed into the Parkside Funeral Home. The absolute saddest, "standing room only" congregation. My parents were barely functioning and so was I. We sat in the front row and listened as Rabbi Schwartz followed our notes. Even hearing him say her name made me feel physically ill. He didn't know her or understand anything about our family but, hey, that's what happens, I suppose, if you leave your house of worship.

When it was all over (and our sitting seven days of Shiva, a Jewish tradition), I went back to my atheism. How could my God or any God let this innocent soul die? Heaven did not need more angels, and whenever someone said that, I wanted to punch them.

I'd just become an only child, which always seemed so lonely. When I'd meet people and they'd ask, "Do you have any siblings?"

I'd pause and decide if I wanted to just say no or be honest and honor Rhonda by saying, "I had a sister but she died." Yes, it was often awkward, but she deserved to always be part of my family. Follow-up questions never upset me. I suppose in an odd, small way, I was mimicking Elie Wiesel when he always said, "Never forget."

My anger subsided over the years, and I tried to be more open-minded about having faith. After marrying my first husband and having kids, we knew the conversation of organized religion would need to be discussed. Brendan was an atheist raised as a Presbyterian. That, plus my Jewish roots, led us to the decision that we would celebrate all the traditional celebrations without the Bible getting involved. Our daughters and our son loved Christmas and Easter as well as Hanukkah and Passover, just as I had all those years as a kid.

And then one day my daughter Kira announced she planned on going on Birthright. It's an organization that provides free trips to Israel for Jews and families of mixed religious backgrounds. Perhaps it was a bit of indoctrination, but the spirit of their mission was lovely. All three of our kids spent two weeks touring all over Israel, steeping themselves in the history and culture. It was life changing. My son, Ryan, was even bar mitzvahed in Mount Sinai. Perhaps, not far from those Ten Commandments?

I started to rethink my stance on organized religion. There were kind and generous people who helped foster this program and for that, I had to be grateful. As my kids start to marry and raise their own kids, I'm sure there will be bar mitzvahs in their future. As the grandmother, I'd be proud to stand on the bema and be a part of this tradition. Because *Hashem Shalee Sandi.*

PANTY RAID

IT WAS A PARTICULARLY HOT JULY MORNING as I trudged up the subway stairs on Third Ave. I caught a glimpse of myself, reflected in a huge glass building on Fifty-Second Street, and I looked *hot*—not the sweaty variety, more of a smoking hot. Twenty-one years old, strutting out of that BMT in a mini skirt, tube top, and platform sandals. In retrospect, I looked a bit like Jodie Foster as a juvenile sex worker in *Taxi Driver.* I was heading to my summer job and feeling like a damn queen. Unfortunately, that feeling faded pretty quickly when I reminded myself that my job was at Herman's World of Sporting Goods in what was loosely called the fashion department. There is nothing fashionable about tennis dresses that have front pockets that brag, "I Have Balls." Also, in my handbag was my lunch, prepared by Greta, in a brown paper bag with a growing grease spot. Not exactly ruling the world.

But on this Friday, I was not going to let my reality get me down because I had a third date with Robert, a law student. Where I come from, a third date means it's time to drop my drawers.

I got to our locker room and cover up my disco-vibe outfit with my Day-Glo orange Herman's smock. Think greeter at Costco, but make it fashion. My boss, Barbara, was already there giving me a bit of her stink eye. This woman did not think I was Herman's material, always complaining about my performance. Barbara looked like Ursula from *The Little Mermaid*. She was just a series of shapes and her hair was always pulled back into a tight ponytail. Her eyebrows were drawn in a high arch so she always looked astonished or cynical. She terrorized me with her constant taunts. "Sandi, why are you so *stupid?!* Can't you do anything right?" That kind of workplace harassment would never fly now, but back in 1979, it was every manager's love language.

And my mistakes? I forgot to put an alarm tag on all the sherbet-colored golf pants. Who would steal lime green golf pants? Then there were rows of sweat suits in bright raspberry and hot pink. The kind favored by my mother when boarding a flight. She claimed it was for comfort. I had this vision of my mother, Greta Handelman, dropping and doing fifty pushups in the Delta terminal.

On this Friday, not even Barbara and her eyebrows were going to yuck my yum. I was counting down the minutes until my lunch break because at the stroke of noon my plan was to cross Third Ave. and go to the Rainbow Shops to purchase that third date underwear. Now, I realize that if a guy wants to get in your briefs, he has zero reason to care about their condition. I could have shown up in my dad's boxers and a bra made out of old rope—wouldn't be a dealbreaker. All of that leg and mustache waxing? It's a waste of perfectly good depilatory.

That is not a deterrent, because I want to nail this date and invest in my future with Mr. "I'm gonna pass the bar exam." I walked inside the store and I'm hit with a gale force wind of air conditioning.

The Bee Gees are on the loudspeaker. Amid racks and racks of beautiful sportswear, I zero in on the underwear. I have entered the magical world of retail Oz. I start thumbing through the racks, looking for my size. I find days-of-the-week underwear, which for some perverse reason I think is sexy. Perhaps reminding a date it's Friday will give a celebratory vibe. I also grabbed lacy 34B bras with a touch of fiberfill. (This is before wonder bras had been invented so the only wonder I could create was a Playtex bra with lift and separation.)

Just as I was about to head into the dressing room, the door opened, bringing with it hot air and a dude who does not look like he's there for a pair of culottes or capri pants. He is trouble. Unkempt, shifty eyed, and wearing a ski jacket—never a good sign on a steamy summer day. He walked toward the cashier and shouted, "Give me all your money. I have a gun and I'll use it!" The poor cashier loses all color in her cheeks. I could tell there had probably been a team meeting about "How to Handle a Robbery," but she wasn't entirely sure she could remember how to handle an actual robbery.

The perpetrator spins around, points his gun at me and a couple other shoppers, and says, "Put your hands up!" So, I do. In my right hand are two pale pink bras and in my left are those days-of-the-week underpants.

Terrified and trying not to cry, I start thinking about what Greta always used to say. "Never leave the house without nice underwear. You never know what can happen." I think she had a fantasy that I'd get hit by a car and the emergency room young single Jewish doctor should see a lady with a modicum of refinement.

I am not wearing the good underwear, I'm holding it! Also, I start thinking about the next morning's *New York Post* article: "Holdup at Rainbow!" Or something cheeky like "Somewhere Over the Rainbow a Shooting Occurred." My mother would undoubtedly give the writer an awful photo of me. These were the thoughts of an unhinged but practical young woman.

In the next moment, two cops arrived on the scene and shout, "Get down on the ground!" So I do. I was lying flat with my cheek pressed to the acrylic high-pile carpet that smelled like cigarettes and disappointment. I could see gum wrappers and old hair ties under those racks. Despite my life being threatened, I was actually disappointed that my Emerald City of a store was a bit of a dumpster fire. At that moment, I heard the sweet song stylings of The Bee Gees singing, "Stayin' alive, stayin' alive!" I softly hummed along as a form of prayer I suppose. I also noticed lots of ankles, because it seemed I was the only customer who was down on the ground.

At that moment the cops yell in my general direction, "Not you, *him!*" Obviously that directive was only meant for the robber. I slowly stood and see he was already in handcuffs.

I was relieved but so shook up that I put that underwear back on the rack. In spite of the danger being already removed from the store, I was still shaking. I asked the cashier how the cops got there that quickly, and she showed me her panic button. I knew that Herman's did not have one of those.

I quickly crossed the street, heading back to work, when something came over me. A snap decision. I knew what I had to do. I was not going to spend one more day working in an environment that was not safe and be bullied by an unhinged boss. Before I could change my mind, I handed my orange smock to Barbara and said, "I quit!" She looked shocked, but I think it might have been her painted eyebrows? I walked out of there knowing I made the right decision. I was broke but free from any impending harassment or a gun in my face.

I've had many work experiences that were less than ideal over the years, but I always had agency over which hazards I was willing to tolerate.

That third date was as I had hoped, in spite of my undergarments. And even though we didn't date long enough for me to attend his law school graduation, I had plenty of opportunities to shop for "date" underwear in stores *with* security guards.

The Casting Sofa Bed

IF ANYONE EVER ASKED, "WHAT DO YOU DO?"
I'd always respond, "I'm a dancer and an actress." I
suppose if you declare a specific career, you might
be magically thinking it will exist. In my case, it
was more fantasy than reality. I would pore through
our trade publications, like the *Backstage* magazine,
to find open calls and auditions that I could go to,
given I didn't have an agent to shepherd my imaginary career.

On one of these occasions, I saw an ad for Hanes
pantyhose. There was an actors' strike, and apparently Hanes needed to shoot a commercial whether
or not the strike was still in force. Being that I was
not a member of Screen Actors Guild and was a bit
desperate, I decided to audition. This was certainly

a bit of a stretch considering the only clothing ad I should have auditioned for was OshKosh B'Gosh (a kids' line of overalls). My legs were and still are short, spindly matchsticks, and unless the brand was appealing to women who wanted to look like Popeyes' girlfriend, Olive Oyl, I'd be an odd choice. But that wasn't going to deter me from an opportunity to strut my stuff.

The day of the audition, I dressed in what I considered the most appealing outfit to show off my legs. If I only had a full-length mirror, I'd have realized I was really being delusional. I had a crop top, a leopard print miniskirt and a pair of fishnets and platform sandals. Hey, it was 1979, and this was a look that would not cause anyone to stare, because everyone was dressing like a disco party was going to pop off at any moment. I wore my shag/Farrah Fawcett feathered hair as high as possible, thinking I'd appear taller. Who was I kidding? I had just moved to the city that year and lived in an old Upper East Side building and the rent back then was $250 a month.

I looked at my reflection on the 6 train and I just looked like a member of the Kars4Kids band. As soon as I walked into the rehearsal studio at the Minskoff Theatre, I knew I had miscalculated my chances. I was surrounded by gorgeous women with long shapely legs and beautiful faces. I was a bristle-headed donkey in a sea of Palomino ponies. A casting assistant had us all sign in, and we were herded into the room in groups of five. The casting director, Jeff, sat behind a huge folding table with a stack of pictures and résumés in front of him. I was immediately taken with him. He was quite attractive, albeit petite and young for a big shot.

I was slightly more encouraged that perhaps he wanted a petite dancer/actress for the job. His feet barely grazed the floor, which I found very endearing. He had the five of us pose à la *Charlie's Angels*. Think awkward gas station calendar, but a short month, like February. After he took a bunch of Polaroids, he told us he'd be calling in a few days if he was interested. Somehow, I knew we connected. I may have imagined a wink in my direction, but remember, I was already a little delusional regarding my chances with my scrawny short "stems."

Two days later, Jeff called. I was gobsmacked that he thought I might book this job and he had me put on hold a couple of dates for the shoot. Then he asked if I'd be interested in going for dinner. Now, I know this is *not* something a legit actress should have considered because that old casting couch trope is an actual problem—so, of course I said yes! If I was willing to work during an actors' strike, I was willing to take my chances on a date. We made arrangements to meet at a restaurant called "A Quiet Little Table in the Corner" where, true to their marketing, every table was in an actual corner. It was very romantic, especially since each table had a circular curtain for privacy.

I wasn't an engineer or an architect, but how was it possible for every table to be in a corner?

Frankly, in retrospect, it looked more like a bunch of office cubicles with breadsticks. But back then, I had stars in my eyes and a fantasy that Jeff, the big shot, was going to launch my career. He would be Nicky Arnstein to my Fanny Brice.

We had a fantastic dinner, and he told me to order whatever I wanted on the menu. To a girl who recently moved out of her childhood bedroom, who rarely went on a date that didn't involve waiting in line at a Sizzler Steakhouse, this was a very big deal. I still remember everything I ordered. I drank Black Russians and had shrimp cocktail (because why would anyone order *that* if you had to pay for four shrimp on a bed of wilted lettuce leaves) and Chicken Kiev. I might mention here that this was not a Russian-themed restaurant, but I managed to eat like Gorbachev.

Jeff told me about his career, casting television and Broadway shows, and I told him about my time at New York University (NYU) and auditioning for musicals. The night flew by, and Jeff, a real gentleman, whipped out an actual money clip that was sterling silver with a money sign on it, very classy, and he paid the bill with what appeared to be ones and fives, but who was I to judge? He then put me in a cab back to my apartment.

A day later, he called and told me the bad news. The strike was ending, but the good news was he wanted to see me again. I brushed off any fantasy of strutting around on a sound stage in a pair of sandal-footed, control-top nude hose and gladly saw him the next afternoon. We went and saw, in the theater, *The Muppet Movie*. We were like two woodland creatures, holding hands and shoveling popcorn in our pie holes, listening to the "Rainbow Connection." I was falling in love. It was a bit curious that with the strike ending he wasn't overwhelmed with new casting assignments, but when I asked, he told me the agencies were gearing back up.

I had a bit of concern when I ran into a dancer pal who also went on that Hanes audition. She told me she had a friend at the ad agency that works on those ads, and they hadn't cast anything nonunion. I thought, *Well, they wouldn't admit they crossed a picket line*, or maybe my friend was a bit jealous that she hadn't gotten a callback. I ignored any potential red flags because I knew Jeff was a sweet, sensitive guy who was unlike anyone I had dated.

A few days later Jeff called and said, "Pack your toothbrush, I have a fun night planned!" We all know the euphemism associated with that "pack a toothbrush" line. It was going to be a sleepover and I was there for it. In retrospect, it makes me happy to know that dental hygiene was important especially since I am currently married to a dentist.

That Saturday night arrived, and Jeff pulled up in a brand-new powder blue Thunderbird. I was a bit nervous, knowing at some point I was going to wind up at Jeff's place, and to be honest, I had no idea where he actually lived. First we had a lovely dinner at Serendipity on the east side and then we headed to his place. We were both nervously chatting as he drove over the Fifty-Ninth Street bridge toward Queens. Now, let me pause here to explain why in 1979 this was problematic. If you wanted to feel like you were heading on the right trajectory, going back towards your hometown wasn't inspiring. Queens (unlike now with its sexy condos, Silvercup Movie Studio, and coffeehouses) was just a borough where immigrants lived until they could afford moving to Long Island or Manhattan. I'm sorry, I'm not trying to offend any of my friends currently living in that borough, but it did not come into its own until around the early 2000s. We kept driving until we reached Kew Gardens. A nice area. I spotted a subway station near where he had parked in case I needed to leave before it was time to brush and floss.

We walked into the lobby of a gorgeous building where the doorman greeted Jeff, and we got in the elevator and rode up to his apartment. He opened the door to a big living area with huge windows. And that's when I couldn't help but notice two older adults, one on a BarcaLounger and the other on a couch covered in a plastic slip cover, watching a movie. I was confused. The woman was wearing a house dress and had curlers in her hair and the man was wearing a pair of bedroom slippers. The woman yelled, "Jeff, if I knew you were coming home, I would have heated up your dinner! Who's your friend?"

Jeff was flummoxed and quickly ushered me into his bedroom. His *childhood* bedroom. I knew this because there were *Godspell* posters and trophies he must have won during a long-ago Little League season. One said "Most Improved," and another was for "Good Sportsmanship." Yikes.

I assumed that Jeff planned our big night thinking his parents would not be home. Any possibility that Jeff might have been kind enough to let his parents stay in *his* apartment were dashed. What was happening? Who was this so-called big shot? All of the little red flags started to flap. We didn't have Google to do any due diligence. But the fact he never seemed to be working and nobody else heard from him after that audition . . . And while a passenger in that shiny Thunderbird, I noticed when looking in the little mirror on the visor, he had rented the car from Avis. I should have asked about it but I really wanted him to be real.

But now, while I watched him open up his fake leather sofa bed and put a Barry Manilow album on his stereo, I was thinking, *This guy is a total fraud.* At that moment I told Jeff he could turn that bed back into a couch because I was uncomfortable with who and what he was. I didn't even want an explanation because he was a skilled con man and could probably think quickly on his feet. Clearly, that audition was pure fantasy. He figured that it was a wonderful way to meet girls. We didn't have

Tinder, Hinge, or J Date, so I suppose it was fairly crafty on his part, but I was not impressed. I told Jeff I was going to leave and take the train back to the city and as I walked past him I thought, *I hope that good sportsmanship trophy is real because I need to safely exit.* Of course, I was still a nice Jewish girl, so on my way out I shouted in the general direction of his parents, "Nice to meet you!" I ran out of the building before he could follow me and got on that subway back home.

The whole ride home I replayed our short courtship and thought I should have listened to my dance buddy. We all now know the expression, "If you see something say something," but the most important part of the message is if you are told something, pay attention. Truth is, I never needed a big shot to shepherd my career. I was capable of doing that on my own and I suppose that deserves a trophy.

Dance 10—Looks 3

WHILE I WAS PURSUING A CAREER AS A dancer, I needed to find creative ways to earn some semblance of a living. I was not qualified to wait on tables because I knew I didn't have the personality required to wait on customers and deliver their food without either criticizing their dietary habits or accidentally dropping an errant baby potato in their lap.

The next best thing, at the time, was standing on the main floor of a major department store like Bloomingdale's and offering customers a sample spritz of perfume. Nobody was interested in my toxic surprise attack, and who could blame them? But a job was a job, and I made the most of it. My favorite company was Christian Dior because the perfume they had me spray was called Poison. What could be more entertaining than sauntering the cosmetics aisle shouting, "Poison for Mothers Day! Get your mom some Poison!" Unfortunately, I was the only one who found this hilarious. The pay was great, I think ten dollars an hour at the time, and I could work as many days as I wanted.

One day, while on my lunch break, I checked my answering service to see if any calls had come in for auditions. This was a time before we had any other means to get messages. There were tons of these services staffed with mature women who I always imagined wore hair nets like a famous Lily Tomlin character, Ernestine the Telephone Operator. I never had any messages, but the operators always spoke as if they were my mother, reassuring me, "It's ok, you will get a message one day." Sure enough, this was that day! I got a message regarding an audition the following morning for the Broadway show, *A Chorus Line*. The company needed replacements for the original cast. I was beside myself. This could be a ticket away from the perfume sample counter at Bloomingdale's, Saks Fifth Avenue, and Lord & Taylor.

I got up the next morning, called in sick, and prepared for the most important audition of my so-called, mostly fictional career. I stuffed my huge dance bag with pictures, résumés, tap shoes, jazz shoes, leg warmers (hey, it was the early '80s), and a water bottle. Tools of the trade. I hopped on the subway and fantasized all the way to Forty-Seventh Street and Broadway about how this audition would get me out of my roach-infested studio apartment and into a one-bedroom apartment with a doorman and air conditioner. I remembered the first time I sat in the audience watching *A Chorus Line* and thinking, *One day, I'm going to be up there, with a top hat and cane, taking a deep bow.*

I got off at my stop and nervously rushed to the theater. It was a hot summer day and the city streets were filled with tourists and locals weaving and bobbing away from the mountains of garbage on every block. A sanitation strike was in full gear and the ratio of flies to humans was probably 1:1. The stench and combination of cigarettes, afore-mentioned garbage, and sweat permeated Shubert Alley. New York City in the '70s and '80s was the Wild Wild West. Crime at an all-time high, a bankrupt city and a government that basically gave up, all were a recipe for disaster. We knew staying safe by being alert and walking in a serpentine motion could prevent a stray bullet from finding us. It sounds dramatic but ask any New York baby boomer and they will concur.

I arrived at the stage door and swung it open with a deep sense of optimism and giddy joyfulness. I was directed to go down into the bowels of the theater and I noticed at least a hundred other hopeful cast replacements. I sized up the competition and did the math. Six roles needed to be replaced and the odds were certainly not in my favor. Positive attitude and a soupçon of ignorance led me to believe this was in my grasp. The dance captain separated us into groups of ten and taught the choreography to the opening number. We each wore a number, like the ones you see at a marathon, and focused and rehearsed until we had those seventy-two counts down cold.

Herded to the stage, I noticed the director, Michael Bennett, sitting in the third row with his dance captain. Star struck, I kept thinking, *Keep it together, do not screw this up!*

The way it works at a dance audition is, after the combination is performed, the director calls your number and shouts, "Thank you!" (which means, sorry but not today) or "Stay" (which obviously means exactly that). I was not thanked for at least six rounds of learning different choreography and the level of euphoria was starting to creep through my bones. I was calculating the Actors Equity scale for a Broadway show and who would I call first with the good news. Next, the dance captain handed each one of us lucky hopefuls sheet music specific to the roles they thought we might be suited for. I was given the song "What I Did for Love," sung by the character Morales, played brilliantly by Priscilla Lopez. Marvin Hamlisch wrote a gorgeous score and even though I was beyond thrilled, there was one minor issue. I couldn't really sing.

I'm not saying I had laryngitis; I was not a singer. This particular song required an actual singer and I could only do my mediocre best in the written key, C. I boldly walked up to the piano accompaniment and brazenly requested a key change and his dead stare told me all I needed to know. "If you can't sing it in the proper key, do your best." And so, I began, "Kiss today goodbye . . ." And that's when I heard from the most important orchestra seat, "Thank you!" Michael Bennett rejected me, but with kindness. After he had thanked me, he mentioned another show he was working on called *Dreamgirls* and that I should try out for that.

Flattered yet flattened with soul-sucking disappointment, I packed up my detritus and headed back out into the humidity and fetid street. This time that stage door swung open feeling like a hundred pounds of failure. I had to shake it off though because I had another part-time job at a local dance studio and I was already an hour late. I had spent six hours in that dark theater and left completely depleted and dejected. Hunger was also an inconvenience because all I had was one five-dollar bill and no time to eat a real meal. I went to a bodega close to Shubert Alley and took out the five to pick up a healthy snack (a Milky Way). But after I pulled it out, it fell onto the sidewalk. At that very moment a young guy, droopy jeans and a dirty T-shirt accessorized with a huge bicycle chain as a necklace, scooped up the bill without breaking his stride and kept loping away.

That was all the money I had, and it had to last me two more days. Something in me started to psychically change. Rage and utter disappointment from the day's events led me to become transformed into a crusader à la Charles Bronson in every vigilante movie. This was not long after New York's new hero, a subway vigilante, Bernie Goetz was getting accolades for taking back what was rightfully his, and I was apparently, at this moment, doing the same.

I started shouting, "Drop it! Now! That's my money, and I have to spray a lot of women with *poison* to get it!" He looked at me, confused, probably because he wasn't accustomed to anyone fighting back and I was continuing my diatribe. A crowd of tourists circled. Instant cameras started to flash and it was becoming that scene in *Young Frankenstein* when the monster is loose in the town square. At any moment I expected to see flaming torches and axes, swinging wildly.

Instead, what appeared was a police officer on a horse. This was a popular NY sight. I have no idea why the police department thought this was a solid plan, but back then it was a basic free-for-all. Drug dealers, porno movie theaters, and high crime rates created an angry circus vibe. The officer dismounted and asked what was the trouble. The kid with my money could not escape because of all those tourists blocking his route, and I explained as calmly as I could that I just wanted my money. Without much prodding, the kid, avoiding eye contact, handed me back my hard-earned cash and left. I suppose the idea of being cuffed and riding on the back of a horse wasn't terribly appealing. The crowd cheered for my success, and the cop trotted off to the next local melee.

At this point, I felt emboldened and fierce. Finally, I had a little bit of control. I could create a new narrative. I flew to Fortieth Street and Seventh Ave. to the dance studio. Powerful and optimistic that this was going to be the new me, I couldn't wait to tell everyone how I took back control and won. It was the salve after losing the most important opportunity of my career. Everyone gathered around as I re-enacted the dramatic events of that afternoon. I illustrated by dipping my hand in my jeans pocket and pulled out that five-dollar bill, and somehow, magically, another five-dollar bill. Now, I had *ten dollars*.

It seems I mugged a harmless kid. I went from victim to perp in that second. Shocked and embarrassed, I could not believe that I blamed an innocent boy and had a block of tourists berate him for retrieving what was obviously *his* money. How? Why? I suppose my utter disappointment and failure caused a level of frustration that transcended all reason.

Ten years later, no longer dancing but instead a talent agent, I was invited to an anniversary performance of *A Chorus Line,* and I wept from the opening curtain until the last bow. I left the theater, where my biggest brush with fame and crushing failure occurred, and all I could think about was that kid and my harsh accusations. I wanted to thank him for giving me a new perspective and my new personal power. If it hadn't been for that experience, I might not have chosen to put away my dance bag and become an agent. I might not have learned that my power of persuasion could be used in a much better outlet.

Nice Girls Finish Last

THERE WERE TWO KINDS OF GIRLS AT MY high school. The good girls were the ones who had a regular babysitting gig, reminded the teacher to assign homework, and always wore their retainer. And then there were the bad girls, also known as hitter chicks. These girls knew how to apply liquid eyeliner, owned an ankle bracelet, and could roll a joint with one hand. These badasses had a bra wardrobe that looked very boudoir ready. I think you can guess which camp I was in.

Let's put it this way, I only wore Bonnie Bell lip gloss and my bras in high school had the word "training" in front. My friends and I hung out on Friday nights in front of the Forest Hills Jewish Center while these sexpots were giving hand jobs behind the Pizza Den. I wanted to be a bad girl like my absolute favorite, Tina Migliacchi, but it wasn't in the cards. Once, while the entire tenth grade was in an assembly, I accidentally brushed against Tina and she got real close, so close I could see tiny mascara clumps, and she hissed, "You are so dead after school!" I was in love. She noticed me. Okay, maybe a playground brawl wasn't a good start to a real friendship, but she noticed me and I took that as a tiny victory.

When it came time for school vacations, my family had us go to places like Washington D.C. or, my mom's personal favorite, Colonial Williamsburg, where we could watch a bunch of local college kids re-enact the olden days. Somehow, watching a girl dressed like a sister wife, stirring a vat of dairy products with an oar from a canoe or eating mutton, wasn't what I would have wanted to experience but, that was my fate. I knew that while I was hanging out with my family in a musty log cabin, at least two of those naughty girls were in Mexico having a "procedure." We all knew what that meant and as awful as the idea was of sneaking out of the country for an abortion (which was illegal in the early '70s), it seemed exciting. Naughty, for my squad, was losing our aforementioned retainer or defacing a bathroom stall with our initials in a heart next to our secret crushes.

"Once a nice girl, always a nice girl" is what I assumed I would be doomed to wear as a banner of my discontent. I tried to break out of this safe branding to no avail. When it came to dating, my friends always set me up on blind dates with nice boys. They came from similar backgrounds—Jewish, good grades, nice families—in other words, a bit boring. Again, this was a time where there wasn't an Internet that had a multitude of dating sites so our friends all did the heavy lifting when it came to matchmaking. I was always pitched as "She's funny and really nice! Your mom will love her!" This was not how I would have wanted to be sold but I guess it was an accurate portrayal.

There was Jeff, med student; Robert, his family owned a chain of hamburger joints; and then there was Larry. True to his description, he was tall, very handsome, and came from a successful family that owned a huge lighting company. He lived in Great Neck, a wealthy community on Long Island, and was very close with his siblings and his parents. My mother was praying this would work out because she had little faith that my nonexistent career as a dancer and an actress would get me out of my childhood bedroom.

Larry was extremely nice and very attentive. At twenty years old, these were not appealing qualities. I know, they should have been, but the heart wants what it wants and at that age all I wanted was to chase a bad boy. Someone who kept me on my toes. Larry and I dated for six months and at that point I knew he was never going to be the one. There was very little spark and, at that age, I expected to be practically in flames. I knew I had to break up with him but one of the pitfalls of being a nice girl is we don't face that kind of confrontation. It's easy to just wait it out until the boyfriend decides it's time to have the "It's me, not you" conversation. If you need to push it, all you have to do is become too clingy or maybe declare your love waaay too soon in the relationship.

It usually worked but somehow, Larry was not deterred by any of my bad behavior. Even those dates I canceled last minute with obviously sketchy excuses. I knew I was going to need to accelerate the demise of this dating situation. Larry and I had a date to see the Islanders play hockey at the Nassau Coliseum and I decided that was the perfect opportunity to break up. It would be incredibly noisy and maybe he wouldn't hear me but I'd still claim I had told him we were over. Or maybe if the Islanders won, he'd be so thrilled the rejection wouldn't sting quite as much.

The night came, I got in his car, and off we went to the game. In my head, I rehearsed what I would say to make him understand it was *me* not *him*. The stadium was packed and, this being my first hockey game, I had no idea how violent it could be on the ice and in the stands. I actually saw a fan rip a metal seat off its bolts and throw it toward a referee. The game was almost over and it was time for me to spit it out. Islanders were winning and I knew it was now or God knew when.

I turned to this big, sweet, beautiful guy and said, well shouted, "Larry, we need to talk!"

He responded, "Yes, we do."

I was thinking, *Oh my goodness, he's gonna give me the breakup speech and I'll be off the hook. I can maintain my nice girl status once again, like it or not.*

This was when Larry reached into the pocket of his "Members Only" jacket and pulled out a small navy velvet box. "Sandi, I know we've only been together for six months, but I love you. Will you marry me?" He proceeded to open the box, and I was staring down a ring that would pay rent for the next five years. This flashlight lit our section of the stadium. It was big enough to cause sun blindness down on that rink. Stunned, all I could think to say was, "No thank you?"

I then softened the blow by reminding him we barely knew each other and our lives were going in different directions. I still pinned my hopes on a career, maybe going on national tours or just finding my way as a gypsy performer, and he was probably going into his parents' lighting business. I mean, if we had married, I could have been up to my tits in dimmer switches, but was that enough for a happy future? Larry was devastated. He could not believe I was not on board with his romantic yet premature proposal.

Then he asked me for a favor: "My parents are throwing us a surprise engagement party tonight after the game. The entire family will be there. It's being catered from Ben's Deli." Ughhh. He needed me to pretend I said yes, wear the Hope-less diamond and act like this was exactly what I wanted. I thought about it for a minute and obviously said yes. At heart, no matter what I wanted to be, I was—and I suppose I still am—a nice girl.

We left the crowded parking lot and wended our way to his home. As soon as we pulled up, there was his mom on their porch wearing a flowery caftan, smoking a cigarette, and smelling like Shalimar waving us in. His dad greeted us inside and gave me a big hug while shouting, "Mazel Tov!" The house was extremely well lit. There were chandeliers and sconces everywhere. It reflected off their plastic slipcovered couches and it was like one of those Ethan Allen showcases. I was overwhelmed by all the cousins and relatives peppering me with questions about our wedding and honeymoon. This was when all my Neighborhood Playhouse acting technique needed to get into high gear. I had to "Yes And" like an improv pro and just tap dance my way through the party. If I had brought my tap shoes, it would have been less of a challenge.

Finally, about an hour later, I told Larry it was time to take me home. I couldn't keep up the charade any longer. We said our goodbyes and had an extremely awkward ride back to my parents' apartment in Queens. I handed back the ring and told him I was really sorry as I got out of his Toyota for the last time. Larry was stoic and still sweet if not still confused.

Ever since that experience, I have tried to be a better person. The thing is, being nice is very different than being kind. If I could be kind, I wouldn't have wound up in a well-lit house, staring down sweaty cold cuts and well-meaning strangers. Kindness means honesty. Telling the truth before things get out of hand could save heartache for everyone.

Pyramid Scheme

AS A DRAMA STUDENT AT NYU, I TOOK GREAT pride in my education. Even though I couldn't afford the tuition (which back in 1977 was less than a week's stay in Daytona Beach), I thought it was the toehold I needed to be discovered.

My parents begged to differ. "Why don't you study something more practical, like nursing?" my mother would ask. Well, considering I could barely pass high school biology and I was afraid of all things that might leak, like blisters, open wounds, or any type of contusion, the recommendation seemed way off brand. Also, my mother was fully aware of my lack of bedside manner. I had a habit of rolling my eyes whenever she started to mutter about her bursitis.

I forged ahead with my schooling until senior year. It was clear, at that point, I was not going to be able to borrow, beg, or hold up a Gristedes to raise the necessary tuition. The only sensible solution? I was going to have to win prize money on a game show. At the time, in NY, there were only two strong options. *Jeopardy*, where you have to not only know things, but also have the ability to answer in the form of a question, and *Ten Thousand Dollar Pyramid*. This was a game where I could definitely do well. The object of the game was simply word association. I had spent the last twenty years associating lots of words!

After doing my research (which, to be specific, was watching the show), I learned that at the end, during the credit scroll, a telephone number was offered to schedule an audition. I called. An appointment was scheduled for the first-round screening and I started my preparation. I treated this audition the way an Olympic athlete trained for the qualifying round. I set my VCR to the daily show and watched every night after class. I also bought the home game version and bribed all my school pals with loose joints and beer to convince them this would be a fun activity. You can get a college student to do *a lot* for some Amstel Lite or weed. I started to sense some of my "volunteer gamers" were beginning to avoid me for fear of a lightning round but I was not to be deterred.

Finally, the first audition was here. I nervously found my way into a dingy office on Fifty-Seventh Street on the west side and there were about fifty other hopeful contestants already in line. I assessed my competition and thought, *These are not serious wordsmiths.* They looked like tourists who were offered free tickets to a television taping for *Maury Povich* or some other daytime shock show. The kind that exposes the real father/mother/cousin/brother. We were all shuffling into a room and seated opposite each other. Edie, the talent coordinator, actually gave us the board game to play. I was ready for battle. My opponent didn't have a chance.

Sitting up at attention, keeping my face as animated as I had noticed the television contestants seemed to be, I spat out one correct answer after another. I had trained myself to the level of a Green Beret, readying for battle. Slowly, wan-nabe contestants were dismissed and I was one of about fifteen remaining hopefuls. Edie announced, "Congratulations! You passed! Please report to the Ed Sullivan theater in one week from today."

Exultant, I skipped my way to the subway thinking about this opportunity. I knew I could find a way to stay in school. Now, the hard work would have to begin. The serious training to close this $10,000 deal. I'd practically sleep with the dictionary under my pillow. If you ran into me on the street and asked for the time, I'd respond, "Watches, clocks, sundials . . ." At the grocery store, if the cashier asked, "Paper or plastic?" I'd respond, "Bags, sacks, things that hold other things." I had become like a walking thesaurus with Tourette's syndrome.

Finally, the big day arrived. The contestants were instructed to wear jewel tones, no black or white, and arrive at the Ed Sullivan theater at 6:00 a.m. Shockingly early, but it had been explained that the staff needed time to prepare us for the taping. I sat on that early train in a meditative state. *Focus,*

focus is going to get me that money, I thought. I had on a bright red sweater with these colorful little wool balls and shoulder pads. My hair was cropped short and, because of my nervousness, I hadn't been eating so I looked and acted like a crack whore with a strong vocabulary.

I arrived at the theater absolutely giddy. I grew up watching *The Ed Sullivan Show* taped in this very spot, a television mainstay, and now the home of my ticket to a diploma. I was led into a huge rehearsal space and spotted a huge coffee urn and a mountain of sugary breakfast treats. Clearly, their mission was to jack us up on caffeine and sugar to get us "performance ready." Then Edie, the talent coordinator, greeted us and mentioned, almost as an afterthought, the show overbooked the week's contestants by one because there is always the chance of either illness or stage fright.

We all looked at each other and thought, *Who is getting the heave-ho?* Not me. Nope. If I had to leave blood on the linoleum, so be it! It had become like a modern-day *Hunger Games* with synonyms. We were once again paired and had to play the game against the rest of these already-screened hopefuls. Thankfully I was told I'd made it and I would be Tuesday's contestant. They shot a whole week of shows in one day, typical of most game shows, and in this case, each contestant only played one day, even if they won their show. I sized up my competitor and knew I had this in the bag.

We filed into the theater, and I was hit by frigid air. Meat-locker cold. I could feel my teeth chatter. Apparently, this was how they kept the audience awake. Perhaps when you see all that mad clapping it's just folks trying to stave off frostbite. Dick Clark jumped on stage, and I was starstruck. He was very handsome, but I noticed he was wearing an excessive amount of bronzer and his sideburns and hairline seemed to have been drawn with a coloring pencil. Perhaps they kept the studio that cold so his face wouldn't start running.

The Monday contestants took their seats, and the game began. A winner was named, another NYU student, and I felt really optimistic. It was my turn, and I got in my seat and met our fellow players who are usually B- or C-level personalities. The holy grail of celebrities on this show was Tony Randall. He starred in the hit television series *The Odd Couple* and was very quick and clever. Unfortunately, Mr. Randall was not there that week. Instead, there was Joanne Worley, whose claim to fame was a variety show called *Laugh In*, and a dude named Sal Viscuso, who played a priest on a hit show called *Soap*. Sal and I shook hands, and the playing began.

We needed to get seven answers in under thirty seconds. Easy. We tore through each category with a perfect score. I was ready for the next step, which was sitting in the winner's circle and answering more words, but this time, at a higher level of difficulty. We could only list the words, not describe them, and our hands were held in these leather straps so we wouldn't give in to the urge to experiment with sign language or gesture. Dick Clark gave me one of his classic back rubs. The first box was revealed. Sal started listing "Seats, pilot, window . . ."

I shouted, "Things on a plane!"

Box after box turned over. I had twenty seconds left to get the last answer. "Mail, a stork's baby," and just as I was about to shout, "Things that are delivered!" Sal simultaneously said, "A special delivery!"

The next thing I heard was a loud honking sound. Because Sal said part of the answer, I was not going home with $10,000. Just $300. And a case of Slim Jims. A guy had one job that day. Just give me clues and not divulge the answer, and he could not fulfill his duty. I was devastated at this loss.

I still had a chance in the next round with Joanne Worley, but unfortunately, she was not a great player and could not come up with the word "totem pole." I was really disappointed. I still can't look at a decorative tribal wooden pole without thinking of that day at the Ed Sullivan Theater. Dick Clark and the audience seemed truly surprised at my loss. The production office offered me an entry-level job, which I suppose I should have considered but the five-dollar-an-hour offer stung too deeply.

I dropped out of school because there just wasn't any other way to raise the funds, and I'm okay with that decision. I learned a very important lesson that day. Luck and chance are wonderful but not something I could depend on for a solid future. I spent a few years after that trying to create a career the old-fashioned way. Earning it without having to depend on anyone's ability to word associate with me.

In Love with My Gay Boss

I WAS SITTING IN THE RECEPTION AREA, nervously buttoning and unbuttoning the top buttons on my blouse. Too many open and I'd look like a cheap tramp; too many closed and I'd look like an angry Mennonite. I was there for an important interview at the J. Michael Bloom talent agency, and I was overwhelmed by all the flash and beauty wandering through the reception area. Even the receptionist was stunning and worthy of her own nighttime network drama.

I kept shifting in one of their leather chairs, hoping my sweaty thighs didn't leave moisture stains when I got up to meet my potential boss. Finally, after what seemed like hours but in fact was only a few minutes, Steven came to meet me with so much flair that I was immediately star-struck. He was about six feet tall, with big blue eyes that were punctuated with a head of prematurely gray hair and a gray mustache. Steven wore a beige linen suit with buckskin shoes to match. Not a hair was out of place nor was his suit wrinkled, which, if you've ever owned linen, you know is quite a feat. He introduced himself, and while he started walking toward his office, he shouted, "Follow me!"

Honestly, at that moment I would have followed Steven to the edge of the world, if it had an edge. He walked as if he was joining the cast of *The Music Man* and had a pool table to sell in River City: confident, playful, and almost lyrical in his nature. He pointed out the file room where all the pictures and résumés were stored, then we passed the copy room, and then we entered his office. I was immediately spellbound and simultaneously in love. You see, I had long ago realized that I am a gay man living inside a straight woman's body. I love everything about the LGBTQ community and have always felt a kinship with gay men. Hell, I took my kids to

Wigstock in the West Village every year when they were still in their strollers.

Steven explained the nature of the job. If I were hired, I'd be in charge of all of Steven's messages, calling actors to go on auditions, talking to casting directors, and running errands for him and his partner in the voice-over department, Karen. It seemed a daunting challenge but I knew I could be an asset as their assistant and eventually learn from these two legends to be an agent too. At first, Steven was not convinced I was the right "fit." I think he thought I was a bit too eager, like that boyfriend who can be a bit too needy. Somehow, probably against his better judgment, he, with the OK from the big boss, Michael, hired me, and from that day forward, my life was infinitely better.

Every morning, I'd get to the office early to be sure to have my proverbial ducks in a row. I made sure Steven and Karen's messages were coherent and that I had called every person necessary to get where they needed to go to book work. Auditions are a numbers game, and to make money for your agency, it's important for the actors to have as many opportunities as possible to get the job. We used to say you'd have to throw a lot at a wall to see what sticks. Not the most glamorous thought, but it was true. I hung on every word Steven said. He was almost like my addiction.

After a few months, when I started to relax and excel at my tasks, Steven took me under his wing to teach me the more essential things to be successful. Who knew that Barney's had a fabulous sample sale at the end of every summer? Steven! I had my first California roll at a local Japanese restaurant with him. This was back in 1985, before you could pick up sushi at your local bodega, when it seemed like the most exotic experience to mix wasabi and soy sauce for more umami. I was becoming his Eliza Doolittle, and I was 100 percent there for it.

After a few more months, I had the privilege to meet his boyfriends and friends. This man was including me in his personal life and the only thing I could give him in return was teaching him the entire opening combination to *A Chorus Line.* Every day during lunch, we'd lock the door and run through it. Popping our heads, doing fan kicks, lots of jazz hands and laughter. It was truly the best of times, and I can still hear us cackling at all of the missed steps and nuttiness of the experience. By year two, I was included at Steven's social gatherings and nights of dancing at exclusive clubs. The world was his oyster, and I wanted to just be anywhere this level of euphoria existed.

All of this started to fray when there seemed to be a mysterious virus infiltrating our clients. It started with Peter. A talented, brilliant, and beautiful actor had called me to say he couldn't make an audition because he had a terrible cough. I didn't think much of it until a few weeks later when he told us he was being admitted to Saint Vincent's Hospital in the West Village because he had pneumonia. We had started to hear about men getting this mysterious pneumonia and knew it was more than that.

First, the experts were calling it "Gay Cancer." Well, that didn't make sense but we knew there was a specific group of patients becoming gravely ill in the gay community. Our technicolor life at work had become sepia, and the fear that our friends could actually die seemed too much to bear. Steven and I went to visit Peter at the hospital and were suited up as if we had been exposed to radiation. Back then, nobody knew how it was transmitted, so there were many precautions taken. Masks, gowns, and gloves were worn for even the shortest of visits.

Walking the halls, we saw room after room of men, frail and pale and in isolation. I believe at that time the entire floor had been dedicated to this mysterious virus. It escalated quickly and we started to lose our clients and friends. Peter died a few months after our visit, and by then it had an official name. AIDS. Dr. Fauci was heading up his team to try and find a cure.

As we all know, it was a worldwide disaster and scientists were racing to find answers. It was like racing to the moon, only far more urgent. We kept somber clothes on standby at work; neatly hung suits and dresses, knowing we might have to attend a memorial service at a moment's notice. The fun and lighthearted lunchtime choreography had ended. Thankfully, Steven remained healthy, but at some point he knew he wanted a career change. Perhaps he thought he might do something that could have him think more global, help more people become their personal best. He became a very successful public speaker and corporate consultant and coach.

I was initially devastated that my first love was leaving me behind even though he had me promoted to replace him. At twenty-six years old, I hardly felt ready to take on his position, but his faith and trust forced me to gain the confidence to do my best. Luckily, I had Karen, a powerhouse in our business, to tutor me in the art of negotiating and networking, and I'm forever grateful for the both of them.

Nothing ever seemed the same after those early years at J. Michael Bloom, but I suppose that can be said by all of us in our journey. A few years after Steven left, I had the good fortune to go out with three other agents and start our own agency. At thirty years old, I was a very proud partner at a thriving business. The first week after we opened, I received a huge wooden crate filled with white tulips. I didn't have to read the card to know they were from my love, Steven. Standing tall, elegant, and proud just like him, with a note that said, "You've got this! I'm so proud of you." I will never forget those early years at my first important job with Steven. I've had many wonderful moments during my career, meeting incredible actors, and still, if I were to say, one of the highlights of my life had to be spending my lunch hour with Steven, door locked, dancing to the music of Marvin Hamlisch and throwing our hands up in the air without a care in the world.

REVENGE

I WAS SITTING AT MY DESK, RIFLING THROUGH a stack of pictures and résumés. It's 1990, and digital is not a word in our lexicon. Instead, I had file cabinets filled with hopeful faces and a list of their credits and special skills. As I worked my way through the pile, I saw her: Amy Seigal. She was unmistakable: same black hair, big black eyes, and black soul. Amy was the Joseph Mengele of my sixth-grade class at PS 196 in Queens, New York. She made torture her favorite pastime back in 1967. And now, I was a partner in a large talent agency with a new last name (thanks to my husband) and Amy had no idea that her hopeful face had landed on my desk.

Without thinking, I handed the picture to my assistant and said, "See this girl? Set her up with an appointment!" And when Adam looked at me with confusion, I explained, "Amy bullied me for an entire school year and revenge is gonna be so sweet!" A big smile crossed his face because Adam, just like most of us theater geeks, had many memories of being mocked or thrown against lockers for our misuse and frequent use of our jazz hands and breaking out into the *Hello Dolly* catalogue in the lunchroom. Let's face it, we had no game and, in hindsight, we were really annoying.

So here was how this debacle all began. My mother got a letter from the local school board the summer before sixth grade telling her that I was going to be transferred to the IGC, which was the Intellectually Gifted Program at PS 196. It was in the wealthier part of our town, which led me to theorize that rich = smart. I know now, with empirical evidence, that is not the case, but when you're a kid and an unmistakable "have not," it's a solid theory.

My mother was ecstatic over this new development. If she had the ability, that woman would have done backflips through our cramped apartment. I, on the other hand, knew this was a mistake. At best, I was slightly above average and I was gonna be a massive and embarrassing failure.

Let's break it down. First, we had terrible taste in our clothes. We shopped in a store in Brooklyn that catered to lower middle-class Jewish families, many Hasidic. It was sort of like Loehmans, the discount store for adults. One big dressing room filled with half-naked adolescent girls. Lots of synthetic stretch pants with tops to match. My shoes all came from a department store called Alexander's, and they were displayed attached at the heel; I suppose it was to cut down on theft, but honestly, no one would risk jail time over these pleather brown loafers. My hair grew horizontally not vertically, so I consistently looked like some sort of isosceles triangle or a very tiny Don King (or for you young readers, Questlove). I had an overbite from being a long-time thumb sucker, and the cherry on top of this shit cake, I had one wandering eye. Apparently back then, the medical diagnosis for this condition was called a *lazy* eye. Ahhhhh, my first awareness that lazy was part of my genetics.

Oh, and then there was the fact that my grand-parents were first cousins, which did not help my situation. So I knew that this new school was prob-ably going to be a disaster. This was one time I wished I had been wrong.

I walked in to the classroom that first day, and I saw a gaggle of beautiful girls clustered in the back of the room, giggling and pointing at me. They looked like baby Stepford Wives, discussing cookie recipes for a Junior League bake sale. Each one of them wore pastel angora sweaters with little gold circle pins, and they had the healthiest hair I've ever seen. The ringleader of this pack of wolves was Amy. I knew at that moment my life was going to be an unending nightmare. My only friend was Hector Grinacoff, who had transferred that year from a school in Chile. His English was limited, but he was obviously very bright or he would not have been as unlucky as I was to be stuck in this chalkboard hell. Poor Hector wore the same brown plaid double-knit sweater for weeks on end. He was always sweaty (that damn sweater), and he had a mild case of what I now know is Rosacea. He appeared to be a very young dock worker with his ruddy sweaty face—and thank goodness he was my friend.

Here is an itemized list of Amy's atrocities.

1. Amy formed the number-one club and invited every girl in our class *except me*. She told me I wasn't a one or a two, not even a three. Thinking about it now, she had it all wrong. I'd much prefer to be identified as a TEN but, hey, tomato, *tomahto*.

2. We played dodgeball at gym every day. Oh, and the gym was also our cafeteria, so while working out, we were also smelling a lot of mayonnaise and old tuna. Amy loved to aim the ball at my face, hoping it would make contact, and yell a victory cheer while shouting, "It's gonna be an improvement!"

3. Mrs. Ostroff, our horrendous teacher (think Nurse Ratched from *One Flew Over the*

Cuckoo's Nest), wouldn't let me go to the bathroom even after I raised my hand, and I peed right there at my desk. I ran from the room in my urine-soaked wool skirt like a homeless tween, and I could hear Amy cackling all the way down the hall. Thank heaven Amy only spent one year in our class because her parents transferred her to a private school the following year. I always suspected that was code for reform school, but that was just wishful thinking.

Preparing for Amy's karmic comeuppance required attention to detail. Like any good soul thievery, the devil is in the details. The day of her interview, I carefully chose my outfit. Back in the late '80s, early '90s, business women and angry divorcees opted for business suits with shoulder pads and pencil skirts. The kind that are so slim, walking up stairs requires a strategy. My hair was blown out to early Farrah Fawcett perfection, and I made sure I had a fresh manicure. I got to my office early and started to rearrange everything on my desk. I had a bunch of framed family photos and a few friendly celebrities in the group, so I faced them out, looking at whoever might sit facing me at my desk. It was a panoramic view of my successful life. My twins, adorable husband, nice house in Scarsdale, and all those aforementioned celebrities.

I also took every Christmas gift I'd ever received at stuck them on my desk. There were Waterford paper weights, Cross pen sets, shake up globes. I wanted the desk to shout, "People like me! They give me crystal thingamajigs!" I then instructed Joanne, our receptionist, to let me know when Amy arrived, but we were gonna let her sit there and stew for a while. Also, my favorite touch, I told Joanne to tell Amy the bathroom was out of order. Ahhhhh . . . the cycle of life.

At this point, I was starting to get nervous. The planning of this escapade was fun, but the reality was not really my thing. I'm a nice person with a healthy dose of empathy. But I needed to shake it off and get my head in the game. The staff all knew what was what. We were all in this together. The meek were going to inherit the earth!

It was go time. Amy had been sitting there for a half hour. I was starting to sweat through my Armani wool double-breasted suit, and I needed this to happen now. My assistant retrieved her from reception and she sat in front of my desk. Nervous (most actors are when meeting an agent or a casting director). I had trouble keeping my mildly trembling hands still. I couldn't look at her so I pretended to be reading her résumé. There was nothing to be read of interest, just her list of acting classes and local theater.

The time had come. I needed to make eye contact. In that moment, I imagined what it would be like to testify in court, facing a perpetrator. She looked exactly the same as her eight-by-ten-inch matte-finish photo, which was how I left her back in the sixth grade. Maybe she made a Faustian pact? We started chitchatting, and it was clear there was zero recognition. I asked her some basic questions like, "Why do you want to do commercials?" And she told me all her friends thought she had the perfect look to sell detergent or diapers.

While she was confidently reeling off all the reasons she'd be a valued client of our office, I interrupted. "Amy, do I look familiar?"

Amy looked confused and answered, politely, "No? I don't think so."

I mean, who could blame her? I did have a new nose and nice teeth, Dr. Lachterman had fixed my lazy eye, and there's nothing like the power of a good hair blower. I responded a bit dramatically (think Joan Crawford) and said, "Does the name Sandi Handelman mean anything to you?" At that moment I knew she knew. It was in her demonic eyes. Fear. Like she fell in a well and Lassie was in another county.

I then continued. "Amy, I only called you here because I was curious to see how you turned out. Obviously, I have done quite well for myself. You see that name on the wall? S. E. M. & M? Well, I'm the last M after the ampersand!" The entire time I spoke like I'm in the third act of a Shakespearean tragedy. In retrospect, way over the top. I could tell Amy was confused, so like the champ she was, she just kept plowing forward, talking about her hopes and dreams. I interrupted and said, "Amy, I have no intention of furthering your career. I just wanted to see you, find out if you have a daughter and if you do, are you teaching her to be as cruel and thoughtless as you were? I wanted you to feel what I felt for an entire school year. Uncomfortable, confused, and disappointed in the lack of humanity. Have I accomplished that?"

Amy told me that I had it all wrong. She pleaded her case saying, "Sandi, we were friends!" I reminded her of all her indiscretions, and that was when it finally sunk in to her feckless head. She could visualize a playback of her cruelty. She quietly apologized, slowly got up, and shuffled backward out of my office. Adam and the staff looked as if they'd just won the office betting pool. They showed restraint and waited until she got on the elevator before letting out a few whoops and high fives.

I wasn't sure I felt that same euphoria. The problem was, I'm a nice person, and revenge and psychological torture isn't really my wheelhouse. I'd like to believe the meek inherit the earth, but that's just something our mothers tell us when the going gets tough. In the real world, especially for a woman in business, meekness can be a big deficit.

It's good to know that someone like me, just slightly above average, could have an opportunity for this sort of cosmic treachery. I'm grateful my grown daughters will have never been bullied or been a bully themselves. I wouldn't want them to ever exact this kind of revenge. But honestly? I have zero regrets.

Hot Pocket

IT WAS A TYPICAL DAY AT WORK, WHERE I was trying not to get busted for being an idiot (which I knew was imminent). I had been working at the J. Michael Bloom agency for two years, and somehow, the big cheese, Michael, believed I had the skills to become an agent. Perhaps it was my gift of gab (in other words, bullshit) that made him think I was an asset to his agency, but I knew it was only a matter of time before I really fucked up. I seemed to have a knack for making money, even if I wasn't great at counting it. I distinctly remember going to the bank to make a deposit and having a teller correct my little deposit slip because I couldn't add. Back in the '80s, we didn't have the convenience of scanning a check from home. Oh no, we all waited in a long line at our local bank to have people do the deposits. It was like going to the grocery store and paying by check. It would take an endless amount of time for the cashier to get that $21.42 approved. Ok, enough of my old timer reminiscing, back to my office.

One day my "bat phone" rang (that's what I called the private line that only our terrifying leader used). One of the reasons Michael was so scary was because he understood that the less he said, the more his employees would blabber. At my initial interview, after Steven gave me the thumbs up, Michael sat behind his huge mahogany desk, sipping his favorite beverage (coke and milk mixed together) while sucking on a menthol cigarette. He had me yammer on about my failed dance career and other mishaps; I knew that this man knew exactly what he was doing. He could expose all my dark secrets without specifically asking. I suppose that was an important ingredient to his success as a negotiator. He also cut quite an imposing figure. His completely white, fluffy hair extended to his sideburns, then connected to his well-trimmed mustache and beard. Somehow, he managed to look like Jabba the Hut, but with facial hair, navy sunglasses, and expensive suits. The man was so much of a character that when the staff surprised him with his portrait by Abe Hirschfeld, it looked exactly like him instead of the caricatures Mr. Hirschfeld was famous for creating. All of this is to say, he terrified me and most of the staff at his highly visible and successful agency in midtown Manhattan.

The bat phone rang and I nervously answered, thinking, *This is the day I'm going to get the old heave-ho.* I already imagined myself packing up my dying plants and office detritus in a small box and being escorted to the elevator, but I couldn't be more wrong. "Sandi, it's high time you take your first big client out to lunch and get her to sign contracts with our agency. You don't want her to go sign with another office! Take her to lunch and get it done!"

Gulp. This wasn't a suggestion but really a dare. I knew if I couldn't make this happen, I would be exposing myself as the fraud I had convinced myself I was. At the time, this actress was starring in a very popular television show called *Kate and Allie*, which filmed in New York. She was considered America's Sweetheart (this was before more sweethearts like Julia Roberts and Jennifer Aniston were on the scene). The actress was Susan Saint James, and I unequivocally adored her. She was talented and kind and she somehow trusted that I could help her get work doing voice-overs and celebrity endorsements. I must have reminded her of either a close family relative or maybe she liked the idea of being my mentor. But I was not going to question her loyalty because I knew that if I could have her sign with us, Michael would be impressed, and I needed that to happen.

The talent agency business is like many businesses, and that meant (and still means) competitive and a bit cutthroat. I was not necessarily either, but my deep devotion and love for actors superseded the rest. I told Michael I was on it and I'd book a lunch spot immediately.

In addition to being terrified of asking Susan to lunch, fearing she'd say no, I was also frightened at the prospect of actually going to a fancy restaurant for a business lunch. I'd never had any meal, up until this point, at a restaurant that had nice cloth napkins and a wine list. Big celebrations in my family meant a night at either the local Red Lobster (where my parents would splurge on special occasions and let me order the "all you can eat" shrimp) or our local diner where my mother convinced me that instead of ordering dessert, I could have the jelly-filled mints at the cash register instead. In other words, my dates and family, thus far, had not exposed me to the life of the ruling class. At the time, there wasn't an internet to research good restaurants near our midtown office, so I had to resort to our Zagat guide book and recommendations from senior staff members.

I finally decided that if Susan agreed to a meeting for lunch, we'd go to a place called Le Cascade. Why? Because it sounded fancy and very French. Oy vey, so ridiculous. The first rule that should be taught in business school is if you are taking an important client to an important meal, know thy restaurant. I summoned the courage to call Susan and ask if she'd like to join me for lunch and she responded, "Sandi, I'd love to!" We picked a day the following week, and I told her I'd confirm a reservation.

Before I lost my nerve, I called Le Cascade and booked a table. It was mid-July, and in spite of a vigorous lunch business back in the heyday of fancy business entertainment, it was an easy time to get into these power places while the captains of industry were already at their Hamptons or Martha's Vineyard compounds. I called Susan back and told her where we'd meet, and she casually mentioned her husband would join us. Gulp. Now I was really nervous because her husband was a titan of broadcast television, literally running part of a network. I might have earned the trust of Susan, but I knew her husband would figure out I was too green and not up to the task of enhancing his wife's career.

I enthusiastically agreed it would be lovely to meet him and changed the reservation for three. All I had to do now was prepare her contracts, figure out what to wear, and pray to God that this lunch would be a success.

New York in July is oppressively hot and humid and my basic wardrobe only had one newish summer dress. I had bought it at an Eileen Fisher warehouse sale and the only reason I could afford it was because it was marked as an irregular. Most of my clothes at the time were slightly askew. It's actually a great way to shop on a budget. The issue with this perfectly lovely white dress with two big front pockets and a dropped waist was that one of the pockets was slightly higher than the other. I solved the problem by slouching a bit to one side to create the illusion that it was some kind of optical illusion. I was fooling no one, but I loved that dress.

I also had a fabulous pair of platform sandals that were called Corkies. They were very popular back then, and they've actually made a recent comeback. I guess, as we all know, everything old is new again. My hair and makeup were pretty minimal back then, and because it was a sticky time of year, my natural head of crazy curls were particularly high and wide.

The day finally arrived, and I nervously walked from the subway to my Madison Ave. office. I started to worry that by that lunch bell, I was going to be a sweaty hot mess in my cotton dress that

appeared wrinkled *before* I'd even left my apartment. I figured it was part of the dress's charm—
hipster chaos? I made sure I put a little marked *X*
next to every page that required her signature and
nervously waited until it was time. I remember
shouts of good luck from other staffers as I headed
to the elevator, and my knees were shaking all the
way down the twenty floors.

Please don't fuck this up was my mantra that day
(and to be fair, pretty much every day) as I walked
the three short blocks to the restaurant on Fiftieth
Street. I opened a huge, heavy wooden door and
entered the lobby that was filled with total glam-
our mixed with serenity and a very judgmental
hostess. There was an actual indoor waterfall that
made me instantly realize why this establishment
was called Le Cascade! I told this sour-faced gatekeeper I had a reservation and she gave me a look
that read, "Are you here to serve someone legal
papers or maybe your boss sent you to bring him
his forgotten wallet?"

At that moment, Susan, already at our table,
stood and waved me in. Thank goodness for the

goodness of America's Sweetheart! I brushed past the front desk and took in my surroundings. Every woman in that restaurant looked stunning. Lots of creamy silk blouses and well-applied lip liner. And the men were in their fancy custom suits. Not one of these diners appeared to have walked more than a foot in the heat that day. It was as if they had been dropped off by helicopter and were taken by a private elevator down to this opulent dining room.

Susan led me to our table, and I could not wait to sit so I could cover my lower body that was not only wrinkled but very sweaty. I introduced myself to her handsome yet stoic husband and immediately knew he knew I was way beyond my depth, but I had to find a way to calm down and hope for the best.

A glass of water magically appeared before me, and I did the unthinkable: I nervously started to chew the ice. Terrible childhood habit and according to my husband the dentist, unhealthy. After a bit of chitchat, our waiter appeared with our menus. Rule number two when it comes to a business lunch: know the menu. Showing up and winging it only works at a wing joint, not a three-star French restaurant. The entire menu (the size of the Magna Carta) was only in French. I did not recognize anything except for one dish: Bœuf Bourgignon. Well, I loved beef, and I certainly didn't know what a Raclette or a Vichyssoise was, so I boldly told the waiter that's what I'd have. Let me remind you, it was a lunch date in *July*, and I had just ordered a bowl of hot mixed meats and vegetables.

My tablemates ordered Poisson, sauce on the side, and I knew that whatever that Poisson was, it was the better choice. Too late now. I noticed that other diners were staring at our table and even though it was clear they were ogling Susan, I felt I was in her heady orbit and just as impressive, sitting there chewing my ice cubes. This was when I began to relax and let my guard down.

Things were going well as her husband, Dick Ebersole, started peppering me with questions. "What can you do for Susan to help her get the right type of endorsement?" I answered surprisingly well, explaining that brands loved her and we were in a position to create good partnerships.

Earnest but not exaggerating, I clearly seemed to know what I was talking about.

Finally, after what seemed an eternity, our food arrived with a flourish. What I later learned were called cloches (these metal hats that cover food) were ceremoniously lifted to display the main event. At that moment, I knew I clearly ordered the wrong thing because the steam that rose could open the pores of an adolescent who hadn't washed his face in a month. Susan smiled as she tucked into her silky fish, and I knew I would have to try and eat without showing my shock that a big, hot, greasy-looking stew was in front of me. I did everything I could to keep my elbows off the table and delicately use my napkin while chatting about my role at the agency.

Just as I got into a rhythm of fork, knife, eat, disaster struck. Somehow I misjudged the distance from the plate to my mouth, and a large forkful of dark meat, pearl onions, baby carrots, and au jous flew into my irregular right pocket. Hot meat and gravy singed the hair on my thigh as the dress slowly looked as if the Exxon Valdez was seeping down my leg. You could smell that unmistakable scent of burning hair, and Susan immediately took charge.

My instinct was to pretend it wasn't happening and pray it away, but not America's Sweetheart! She quickly summoned the waiter to bring a glass of club soda while she simultaneously helped me by digging into that poor pocket and scooping out the baby vegetables and steaming meat. Horrified, I excused myself and grabbed my napkin to hide what now looked like a miscarriage and slink to the ladies' room.

I thought, *At this point I've ruined way more than this permanent markdown irregular dress. My career will be over before it had a chance to begin. Those contracts in my bag, pulsing throughout the meal, will never get signed, and I'll be back to being a receptionist at some sad law office.* I walked into a very elegant and thankfully quiet bathroom, empty except for a bathroom attendant. This used to be a popular perk in fancy spots. A woman, who in this case seemed a bit disgruntled, would sit on a chair ready to offer hair or face cream or bobby pins, tissues—all the stuff that fancy ladies might require to "freshen up."

It was obvious to her that I needed a lot more than freshening, and she wanted no part of this daytime nightmare. I quickly turned on the faucet and started to dump the remaining food out of my pocket. Sadly, this was an old sink with a very small drain opening, so it required me to push the baby corn and pearl onions down that drain one by one and pray they didn't start to clog up the works. Oh, important detail, I had lifted this cotton dress to my waist to get it somewhat clean so if anyone happened to walk in, they'd get quite a show. Naturally, my underwear wasn't what you'd want to see before you ordered your crème brûlée, and I prayed I'd be in there alone as long as possible.

After I got the dress somewhat clean, I then needed to dry it, and my only option was one of those heated hand dryers. The challenge was getting my dress up as high as this impossibly high dryer. Maybe the restaurant's architect had decided if you could afford to eat here, you'd be over five foot six. I had to lift the dress over my head to get it dry, and now it was a full complement of my undergarments and it was not pretty.

All this time, the attendant just stared, knowing I wasn't carrying my handbag, so whatever damage I did to her otherwise pristine domain would not be rewarded.

Finally I was dry enough to walk back to the table. I prayed that Dick hadn't paid the bill and left, and I saw they were still there. Susan joked about the experience, and that's when she asked, "Don't we have contracts to sign?" This absolute queen knew how nervous and embarrassed I had been and defused the moment by being herself: perfection. I grabbed the contract and opened it to the signature page and noticed a little gravy stain. We laughed while Susan signed and said that we'd always remember our first contract.

I will never forget that day and the confidence she gave me. This was exactly what I needed back then so I could stop beating myself up for being green, in the weeds so to speak, but most important, willing to learn from the kind of people I could respect and value. We spent many years working together, signing longer term contracts and making money together, and I have maintained that the key to my success was to understand doing well could mean working with people who could have mutual respect; I could treat them like family, and they would reciprocate. Working hard in any high-pressure business requires more than a business acumen and a pedigreed education. I have learned it requires earnestness and a big heart. I'll always be grateful for the opportunity to learn from my mistakes and will never order a bowl of hot meats for a summer lunch again.

BEND AT THE KNEES

I WAS LYING ON A HOSPITAL BED AT AN eighty-degree angle. My head faced a disconcerting amount of debris on the linoleum floor. Gauze pads, tissues, and discarded syringes did not make me feel confident that I was in a healthy situation. I was here was because, pregnant with twins, my water has broken ten weeks too soon. Apparently, if that happens, the baby (and in my case, litter) needed to be born, pronto.

Terrified, I stared at my swollen bare feet that resembled unbaked Cinnabons, and I kept thinking, *Why me?* There was a lot of busyness around me. A few maternity nurses, my obstetrician, and Brendan, the most nervous dad in waiting, all buzzed about. Poor Brendan kept trying to rub my shoulders, and I kept swatting him away. We only managed to get to our Lamaze class twice, so all we had learned thus far was "offer to rub your partner's back and breath." Oy. Not helpful during this shit show.

One of the nurses started drawing my blood and Brendan passed out. All of the sudden, the medical team was tending to my fragile husband while I was in a painful, way-too-early labor. How did I get in this pickle? Well, we all know the biology, but this was not what I had expected while reading *What to Expect When You're Expecting*. After thirty-six hours of this insanity, all the monitors started ringing. It was like I'd gone through an airport metal detector with a Glock in my handbag. The umbilical cord was tightening around Twin A's neck, and those teeny girls needed to be out STAT.

Within seconds, tracing paper and a marking pen were prepping me for surgery, and all I could think of was whether my doctor would remember the anesthesia. Thankfully, within a minute or two, I was unconscious, and those preemie nuggets were born. They had all their fingers and toes and screamed like champs even though they were, combined, under five pounds. They resembled tiny gerbils in their incubators. They were so tiny they couldn't wear preemie diapers, so the nurses put them in face masks. Nothing like staring at babies in what appeared to be string bikinis.

I recovered from the surgery and had the misfortune of leaving the hospital with a basket of flowers and no babies. They were doing well but needed to grow until their due date in the hospital. Every day, I'd go visit them and bring my breast milk, which was fed to them through a small tube. Every once in a while, their baby monitors would ring while one of the girls was having an apnea or bradycardia and we were instructed to shake them to get them restarted. Can you imagine having to reset your baby? I was constantly terrified that I would not be able to "restart" one of them. I kept wishing my sister was alive because she would have been able to calm me during this most stressful time.

Seven long weeks of watching them grow like chia pets gave me a lot of time to fantasize their homecoming and how exciting it would be to visit all their cousins and my family. Despite being back at work and getting little to no sleep when they did get home, I started planning our first trip. I had decided that at a year old, Kira and Lindsey would be ready for a cross-country trip to see Brendan's family in Palo Alto. The hubris of a new mother with zero understanding as to what's involved in traveling with a pair of high-strung babies! I had this notion that flight attendants and other passengers would be so taken with their cuteness that they'd all pitch in during the flight.

Maybe it was the fact that Kira had a five-hour snot bubble and Lindsey smelled like old yogurt, but there were no volunteers. By the time we disembarked in San Francisco, I believed flies were beginning to swarm from the stench. We collected all of our luggage and baby paraphernalia and limped like wounded soldiers toward the exit.

As soon as we got into the bright sunlight, I saw Audrey, Joe, and their two toddlers standing next to their minivan waving at us. They were tidy and organized with a clean van. We, on the other hand, looked like one of those National Geographic pictorials of tornado survivors. Disheveled, exhausted, and covered in unidentified stains. My diaper bag had a thin coating of powdered cheese from the twins' Pepperidge Farm Goldfish crackers and empty juice bottles. Before we even got to their beautiful home, Audrey handed out an itinerary for our five-day visit. We would spend a day in Chinatown and take a trip to Santa Cruz and the Rodin Sculpture Garden at Stanford. I got vertigo just listening to the schedule.

Their house was perfection. There were only wooden toys and the smell of baked goods wafting from the kitchen. Compared to them, we are raising wolves in a henhouse. Slowly, we found a way to acclimate, but it was not easy. Kira and Lindsey had no desire to show off their cooperative skills or healthy sleep habits, so we just counted the hours until we could go back to New York. Somehow, we rallied and manage to stroll through the lovely streets of San Francisco and those Rodin gardens, but on day four, both the girls got ear infections and were running fevers, so we decided to skip Santa Cruz.

After a visit to Audrey's family pediatrician, the girls started feeling better, and we decided on a pleasant walk to their local playground. The men stayed behind to prepare for watching the World Series. Finally, I felt like I could relax and enjoy our visit while pushing the girls on swings. At that moment I heard a loud rumble, like the R train running beneath us. I looked up and saw the road in front of the playground buckling and, at that second, Audrey shouted, "EARTHQUAKE!"

I pulled the girls off their swings, and we jumped into a sandbox. Their stroller traveled to the other side of the playground, and we watched in horror as cars were rocked off their axles. After what felt like an hour, but was in actuality thirty seconds, it stopped. Slowly, we brushed ourselves off, calmly found our strollers, and made a hasty exit for home. All four of the kids were fine and oblivious to what had just happened. When we arrived back at their house, we saw the guys sweeping up broken glass and all those wooden toys. When the news came on, the coverage was terrifying. The bridge that would have taken us to Santa Cruz had collapsed.

Minivans, just like Audrey and Joe's, were crushed. I started to cry thinking of what could have happened to my family. Somehow, we managed to get the first flight out a day later, and I was never happier traveling with my messy, untamed family than that day.

It took me a couple of years to recover and travel back out west, but I finally decided it was time to have a girl trip and see a good friend, Leslee, in Los Angeles. I missed being with my children, but I knew I needed a break to do some of my own resetting. On the last night, while I was thinking about how much I missed my family and couldn't wait to get home, I heard that unmistakable sound of the subway. When I looked at the ceiling in Leslee's guest room, I watched as her ceiling fan started bobbing, looking as if it could fly toward me. I knew it was another major earthquake.

It was four in the morning, and Leslee and I were wandering the streets of LA looking for an open coffee shop. Shock and awe can make a girl do the illogical. Thankfully, we were not harmed, and her apartment just had minor damage. Two days later, I was back on a flight home. All I could think about after all those unexpected surprises (early babies and two big earthquakes) was how random life can be, and the best advice I can offer is bend at the knees and hold on to a handrail because life will try and shake things up at any opportunity.

Wedding Bell Blues

EVERY MORNING, MY ASSISTANT, ADAM, would leave a few stacks of my mail organized on my desk. There would be the pile of pictures and résumés, personal mail (before email, correspondence came in an envelope with a postal stamp), and then a pile of miscellaneous invitations. The invites were mostly from actors who wanted the agents in my office to attend their performances. Again, no Facebook, Instagram, or other delivery systems to strut their stuff.

On this one particular morning, I noticed on top of this organized chaos a thick, creamy envelope with my name and address in a gorgeous calligraphy. The kind that always made me think I'm being summoned to Thomas Jefferson's son's bar mitzvah.

Lots of curlicues and dainty script that, in this case, said, "Sandi Marx and family." I love getting invitations. I think it's partly because my childhood did not include many of these thick, fancy, engraved invitations—or any invitations for that matter.

It was well-known at my office that I was the good time girl, the designated party attendee. My partners were all ten years my senior, and the last thing any one of them wanted to do during their sacred weekend was attend a wedding, a bar mitzvah, or a baby-naming ceremony. They would roll their eyes and RSVP their regrets. But that was not me, oh no. The best way to describe my stance on these occasions was to pack some metaphorical confetti in my pocket for additional joy and celebration. There was a popular ad in the '80s for Life cereal where a bunch of kids would shout, "Get Mikey to try it! He'll eat it! Give it to Mikey." At my agency, I was Mikey.

I opened this heavy stock envelope and was thrilled to see that my family and I were invited to David Cooper's wedding. A lovely actor and voice-over talent, he was throwing a big party at his home on Long Island in July, during the day. I was thrilled because this would be the first opportunity I had to show off my two-year-old twins to clients and other industry folks who hadn't met them. Additionally, this could be a nice bonding opportunity for Brendan and I to have a long car ride to hopefully connect, since there was very little connecting at this point in our marriage. Our conversations were mostly regarding the kids, our bills, and who didn't remember to turn off the lights in the kitchen.

Our relationship had devolved into Brendan leaving me a punch list every morning of chores and items that needed to be attended to. I had become a bitter intern in a life I had fantasized all through my obviously naive childhood.

Also, a day and night of celebration would only cost us gas and a gift, both expenses I could have my company cover. This was going to be great. First hurdle, before my emphatic yes with hearts and flowers on that RSVP card, was clearing it with Brendan. I knew he would not be thrilled at the prospect of giving up a summer Saturday to drive to the east end of Long Island in beach traffic when he could be trimming our hedges or repainting our deck. As a side note, one of our most toxic fights happened on a hot summer weekend when he told me I should be vacuuming rather than taking our kids to our local pool. To this day (please don't judge), I have not operated a vacuum cleaner. Maybe I have dust busted but that vacuum needs to be operated by anyone else but me. Trauma is real.

I figured the best tack to take was wait until he was in a good mood (a rarity for sure) and casually mention that it would be a lovely way to spend the day together. I also had been reading lots of magazine articles on how to rekindle a relationship and going out on dates to try and reconnect, to remember the fun we used to have being frivolous. I knew that was my ammunition, so after a bit of prodding, he agreed. Relieved, I mailed the RSVP back and started planning our big outing with the girls. I wanted them to look their absolute best and that meant fabulous outfits. Even though it was a backyard wedding, these girls were gonna be tricked out as if it were a coronation.

I searched everywhere in the city for the perfect dresses and found them at a store that catered to brides and their flower girls. The dresses I picked were multi-layered, ruffled, and had little pearls adorning each tier—puffy and bright turquoise for Kira and pink for Lindsey. I knew they would look like princesses. Then I found them black patent-leather Mary Janes (shoes with ankle straps) and ruffled white socks. They weren't quite walking yet, but I was not raising hobos. They were going to be wearing shoes.

As soon as I got home, I wrestled them into these outfits, and they looked like they were heading to their quinceañera. They were beautiful, and I thought I nailed it.

The Saturday finally arrived, and it happened to be a very hot and humid day. I watched as Brendan dragged his feet to get on his suit, and I found a summer dress that would be nice enough and comfortable. I then loaded our car with all the provisions necessary for a long drive, including lots of snacks, juice bottles, and diapers for the girls. I got them strapped into their car seats, smoothed their rows of starchy ruffles, and sat shotgun. I had decided that as soon as we hit the highway we would put on their favorite music and as they dozed, Brendan and I could talk—uninterrupted!—about anything except the kids or household stuff.

This was before we had navigational tools for driving, just a paper map. Our map had been folded and crumpled so many times it was barely legible, and to be honest, I couldn't figure out how to read a map even if it had been pristine. We were heading to exit 65 on the LIE to a town called Yaphank; if there hadn't been traffic, it was an hour and a half away from our Scarsdale home. I failed to mention this detail to Brendan, fearing he'd say no. I'm not proud of this minor offense. I justified it to myself that I was trying to save our marriage. Maybe a misdirection, but at that point I was desperate.

Everything was going smoothly; girls had fallen asleep, and we turned the radio to more adult music and both started to talk like a pair of adults that liked each other. We passed towns with optimistic exit names like Utopia Parkway, New Hyde Park, and Springfield Boulevard. All names that bring to mind a bucolic setting and the American dream. Just as we got to exit 39, Great Neck, both the twins started crying. I quickly found fresh bottles, but that did not calm them down. On closer inspection, I noticed they were both covered in bright red blotches. Apparently, those frilly dresses were made of synthetics that had no business touching the delicate skin of our two-year-olds.

Their diapers were very full after all those bottles. I realized that with diaper rashes and hives we'd have to escalate this wardrobe malfunction. I quickly told Brendan to pull off the highway and find a service station so I could buy children's Benadryl and change their diapers. These poor girls no longer looked angelic—more like Madame Alexander dolls that had been dragged around for way too long. You know, those creepy dolls that only have one operational eye lid, a blank winking menace.

I instructed Brendan to go inside the Mobil station and find the liquid medication while I found a bathroom. This was an old gas station bathroom that probably hadn't been attended to in a few months, but that was not a deterrent. Desperate times called for desperate measures. I laid a changing mat on the tile floor and quickly got to work. Their diapers were both extremely heavy and so wet they had seeped through to their fancy dresses. I hadn't thought to bring a change of clothes because I was so focused on them looking like baby royals, and now they looked like they were ready for a walk, really a crawl, of shame.

After getting them cleaned up and dosed with the antihistamine, we were back on the road. Gratefully, they fell back asleep and within a half hour, their rashes had subsided. At this point neither I nor Brendan were in the mood for date day conversation. I could tell he was thinking it was my fault they had a reaction to their clothes, and to be fair, he was 200 percent correct.

An hour later, after stop-and-start traffic, with most cars filled with families heading to the beach, we got closer. The exits seemed more foreboding, like Amityville and Babylon, but finally we found our way off the highway and toward the party. I was concerned that we might have missed the ceremony after our detour, but I knew no matter what, David would be touched that we actually made it.

We drove to their street and found a parking spot almost immediately, which I took as a positive sign. Like a good omen that the rest of the day would be a delight. I started to unstrap the girls' booster seats when Brendan asked why there were no other cars on the block. I figured they'd hired a valet who put them somewhere else, but then I saw David through his kitchen window washing dishes. Why, on his wedding day, would he be in his kitchen? I quickly grabbed the invitation and carefully read it. I could barely speak when I saw the date of the party. It was for Sunday, not Saturday. We came a day early. Panicked, I threw both girls back in their car seats. I handed Brendan the invite, and the look on his face was not what I had expected. He started to laugh, and, in turn, so did I. I was so embarrassed, I couldn't bring myself to ring their bell and drop off their gift. I just rushed back into my seat and shouted, "Drive!"

We didn't have cellphones, so I waited until we got home, two hours later, to call David and tell him my mistake. After a profuse apology, I made David swear he would never tell a soul what had happened. The last thing I wanted was for my clients to think I was a disorganized mess, which I clearly was at that time.

He kept his word, and it was many years later, after I had retired from being an agent, that I was ready to share this story.

In spite of Brendan's good humor that hot afternoon, my plan to reconcile things on the Long Island Expressway never did get back on track. But not from a lack of trying. I would also be lying if I told you I learned to always double-check dates and times on invitations. But honestly, if a disgruntled husband could forgive me that summer afternoon, then I could forgive myself.

And those toxic dresses were never worn again.

Holidays Are
for Regifting

BRENDAN AND I HAD BEEN MARRIED FOR A few more years, and the challenge continued. I am going to preface this story by saying that in the last five years or so, I have adopted a posture that includes having grace and kindness. We have all heard that expression, "There are three sides to every story when it comes to relationships: each of the partner's sides, and the truth." That said, here is my truth, shared with grace. Okay, now that I got the preamble out of the way, this is a sliver, a slice of crumbled apple pie, if you will, of what actually happened back in the mid '90s.

Brendan and I had been married for five long, arduous years, and we were both putting in the effort. That will already tell you things were not going great. We were blessed with our twin daughters, who, in spite of their early arrival, were thriving, and we had settled into a good life. It was one that I had dreamed of ever since I could remember. We were still struggling financially, and since we bought a house we could barely afford, that also meant two cars and a decent private nursery school. But we managed to do what was necessary to keep this overextended circus on track.

The Christmas season was approaching, and this was a particularly big part of the Marx family tradition that I loved. Being raised with just a handful of Chanukah gelt and a few sad presents did not hold a candle (no pun there) to his family's huge adorned tree and stunning dinner, replete with a shiny ham and lots of crudités. I was certainly looking forward to all the festivities but was feeling the pressure of having to buy gifts for all the nephews and Brendan's sisters and brother. Then I had to consider appropriate gifts for his parents, Pat and Roland. Lovely to a fault, but very different than my parents. Well-read and traveled, they were extremely sophisticated. My mother would call them the unclassiest of words, classy. The pressure was on.

We both worked long hours, and when we got home, we were alternating between the caring and feeding of our four-year-olds and fighting with each other. Oh, and did I mention I was pregnant? Nothing like trying to solve marital discord by having another baby. I'm still, all these years later, astonished that we had the energy or romantic inclination to have that happen.

I needed to adopt a strategy to prepare for this big Christmas event. In the early years of our marriage, I was preoccupied with winning the affection of his family by trying to assimilate. Gone were my spandex jumpsuits and platform shoes, replaced at these gatherings by my favorite Laura Ashley dress that had found tremendous popularity in the early '90s. I had transformed my *Dance Fever* image to a faux prairie bride. Puffy sleeves and a bow in the back of my dress that skimmed my calves, let's just say it was quite a pivot. I figured if Martha Stewart could wear this dress on the cover of one of her hostessing books, so could I.

I needed a game plan to be seen by his family as an asset to the Marx name. Of course, this was a completely self-imposed challenge because they did like me, but I think they liked me as sort of a novelty. His mom loved to pepper me with questions like, "How do *you* prepare your bagels?" As if my Jewish heritage held some family secrets regarding a toaster oven and a swipe of cream cheese. They served their bagels with salmon, lemon, and capers. My mother wouldn't have known a caper if it was in her mouth. And it was lox in our kitchen, not salmon. I know potato, *potahto*.

This was my plan. Go to Toys R Us and get the children toys and books—easy and not prohibitively expensive. The adults were another story. How do you shop for conservative yet cultured adults who love anything from the Museum of Modern Art bookshop or a Lands' End catalog? I came up with a brilliant solution: regifting. Nowadays it's considered the right way to gift, ecologically responsible and hip; but back then, not really the case.

As a talent agent I had been given a closet full of fabulous gifts just ready to be moved into their next home. There were sterling silver pen sets, crystal paper weights, perfume, and (my favorite gifts) huge art books. The coffee table book was ubiquitous, and everyone I knew (including myself) had several casually stacked on their shelves or coffee tables. One of my clients, Barbara Feldon (brilliant, talented, and generous), gave me a book called *A Day in the Life of Pictures*, and as much as I loved it, I already had a copy. This was the perfect gift for my sister-in-law because she was an avid photography buff and I knew I was gonna nail it.

We wrapped all the gifts the night before our trek to their gorgeous home in Mill Neck, Long Island. As I carefully wrapped regifted cashmere scarves and desk accessories, and the kids' toys, I felt victorious. I had cracked the Christmas code. Even Santa would have been proud of my handiwork.

The next morning, we loaded the kids, all their paraphernalia and a huge sack of those gifts in our car. Even though Brendan and I had been fighting, I had a sense of optimism. In spite of our shaky marriage, I was excited to have another baby, especially since—after having a high-risk pregnancy with twins—a singleton birth would be a walk in the park.

We finally arrived, pulling up the long private driveway to their house, and unloaded everything. Based on everything that came out of our car, it was like moving out of a studio apartment with a U-Haul. You'd think we were planning on staying a week, not the one night that was on the schedule. But once we got unpacked, everything inside was heavenly. The smell of meats slowly roasting in the kitchen, the pine tree that had been beautifully adorned with red ribbons to acknowledge the AIDS crisis (yes the Marx family was liberal minded), and the classical music in the background. All that was missing was snow and Bing Crosby making an appearance.

Roland served champagne and caviar while the cousins all tore through the house, playing tag, and I felt, momentarily, very lucky. This was what I always hoped for. A Hallmark holiday without guilt. I had finally assimilated! Even if I was convincing myself this was what I wanted, I was willing to give myself this tiny triumph. The Marx tradition was to open all the gifts before the sumptuous meal and we assembled in the living room. The children all tore through their wrapping paper, and Pat collected every scrap so she could save the paper for a future project. Maybe she'd build a papier-mâché dollhouse? Who knows, this woman was so talented, she made her own pâté from scratch! (In my experience, it was called chopped liver and was not formed into a loaf, so I was in awe.)

Then it was time for the adults to open their gifts. Manners and tradition meant slowly unwrapping and always reading the cards first. This was something I needed to concentrate on getting right because where I came from, we savagely tore off the wrapping as if it was a time bomb ready to detonate.

Ooohs and ahhhs were echoing after each subscription to the *New Yorker* and cashmere sweater from Brooks Brothers were opened. And then the big moment, Nancy was opening my gift, the big book. I could hear my heart beating in my chest. It could have been gas from all the pâté, my gestating belly, and club soda, but I focused on her reaction. She held it up for everyone to see and I knew I nailed it. She then proceeded to open the book and started to read the inscription. Wait, I didn't remember writing one. I had given her a card—what was happening?

She started to read out loud, "Dearest Sandi, thank you for a fabulous year and all your hard work. Can't wait to see what the new year brings. Love, Barbara."

Oh my goodness Jesus. Oh shit. Fuck. I now could feel my ears get hot and I started profusely sweating under my boobs. I'm sure there were smile wet marks on my dress. Pregnant, swollen, and now sweating like the pig that was on convection in the Marxes' oven.

I had to think fast. Obviously I was caught regifting. But if nothing else I was a survivor and good at thinking on my feet so I quickly responded, "Yes! Barbara gave me that book and, since I already had a cherished copy, I thought of all of my friends and relatives that *you'd* appreciate it the most!" I saw, from the corner of my eye, Brendan giving me one of his death stares, but I ignored it. The rest of the family, awkwardly ooohed and clapped and Nancy, gracious as always, seemed to love it.

The rest of the night went fine and the tension between me and my husband seemed to be our secret. Our drive back home was uncomfortably quiet. I put on the kids' favorite Raffi songs and started to think more and more that I was living in someone else's narrative. I had already changed my appearance, vocabulary, and countenance for a man and his family that seemed like the fairy tale I always hoped for. The thing was, a real life fairy tale meant you were happy and supported being who you truly are, not conforming to someone else's ideal.

I am grateful we stayed married long enough to have my precious son and really tried to make it work, but when it became too arduous, I knew it had to end. Things came to a head one night during one of our fights that escalated quickly when Brendan hurled a diaper toward me that had been sitting on Ryan's changing table. This weapon was filled with hours' worth of my mildly neglected son's detritus.

In other words, lots of pee, poop, and what appeared to be fiberglass. If you have three kids, diapers do not necessarily get changed on a regular basis. Hey, it's not only economical, I'm . . . doing my part to save the environment?

It landed and exploded right at my feet, and that was the absolute last straw. I told Brendan, "If we don't see a marriage counselor, this is not going to end well." He agreed, probably worrying about how I could retaliate after the toxic diaper incident.

We went to a marriage counselor named Dr. Choubilier, who Brendan dubbed Dr. Chernobyl. I of course called him Dr. Chevalier like the French film star. Not to oversimplify, but this was a prime example of the root problem of our marriage: Brendan was a serious and introverted thinker and a brilliant and a fantastic father, but he and I were not compatible. I preferred being the village idiot. I was happy to watch David Letterman to unwind, but he'd rather read about black holes. In what I still consider unprecedented, our therapist told us not all couples are meant to be together, and I took that as a permission slip to do the hard thing of calling it quits.

Kira and Lindsey were eight and Ryan was barely four. It was excruciating and exhilarating in equal measure. We had a very civilized divorce and shared custody. I could finally breathe in a way I hadn't in a long time. I could wear something inappropriate if I felt like it and not always be on guard for my questionable grammar. I made a choice to have my kids grow in a home with a strong independent mother. I love Brendan more today than I ever had while we were married. Our mutual respect and appreciation for each other has evolved over the past twenty-five years we've been apart. I miss those Christmas dinners and all the fancy pageantry as well as his lovely family, and I'm grateful I have those eight years held now as a memory. Sometimes when I'm in a gift shop, I'll spot a big coffee table book, and I think of Nancy and her grace. Remember, there are three sides to every marriage, and the most important side is the one that brings peace.

HEAD ABOVE WATER

I STOOD ON THE EDGE OF AN OLYMPIC-SIZED pool. There was Kate to my right in her shiny red speedo suit, hair pulled back in a high ponytail, and to my left was Cricket, impossibly thin (probably had crickets in her diet, which would be why she was known as Cricket), with bright blue eyes and a delicate nose. I was in the middle with my rat's nest of hair in a black tankini that was supposed to be a bikini! But I was a mom! My cottage cheese ass would tell a different story. I was visibly shaking because, somehow, I was supposed to jump in a body of water and swim to the other side. Why? How had this happened? I had no business being in this self-made predicament. But this is how the debacle came to be.

After our daughters' second Christmas, living in our cramped New York City apartment, we knew it was time to move to the suburbs. As much as I absolutely loved living on Manhattan's Upper West Side, it was not ideal for two toddlers. There was a big Christmas tree in our lobby with gift boxes as decorative props, and Kira and Lindsey thought this was their tree as they tried to open those gifts. Our building didn't have a play area for them, so this was their only option in the winter for entertainment.

Brendan thought Scarsdale would be a wonderful place to raise a family, and I was a very enthusiastic, two thumbs up. The only references I had for this bucolic suburb were television shows and plays where Scarsdale seemed to be the place where the upper-middle-class parents lived and also where a famous diet doctor had been shot by his lover. Jean Harris, the perpetrator, was a headmistress at a private girls' school, so I thought even the murderers were fancy. I wanted a fancy life and to give my kids something I never had: their own bathroom and a front lawn.

I didn't think we could afford to live there, but somehow, between the two of our salaries and a large bank loan, it became a reality. We found a house that was not attached to another, had a drive-way, hedges and a powder room in the front hall. I never imagined I'd need a bathroom for freshen-ing up my face, but sometimes the unimaginable can become real. It was a very exhilarating time. All of our apartment furniture fit in one room, and we knew that, over time, we'd fill the other seven rooms with beds, dressers, and (hopefully) lovely wool rugs. The kids were thrilled that they could tear through the living room on their little trikes and not careen off walls or corners.

After we settled in to our new life, it became clear that I needed to make friends. Since the girls were not ready to go to school, there were few opportunities for me to meet other moms at school pick-ups and drop-offs. Also, as a full-time work-ing mom, I wasn't in the neighborhood during weekdays. Our babysitter would take the girls to the playground, but that didn't really foster oppor-tunities for me to meet women, just stay-at-home moms who tried to poach our nanny. It is a dog-eat-dog world in childcare.

Luckily, I did meet a slew of fabulous women on the 8:21 train to Grand Central Station, and these women are still my friends. We formed a bond, thirty-one minutes each morning, mostly complaining about our jobs, husbands, and children. I was living inside a John Updike novel. Hooorah!

At some point, after being in our suburban life for a few years, I decided I needed to be more intentional about making friends. My first tactic was sitting on our front "stoop" (which was really just a little step) and wait for other moms to walk by. This didn't really happen because the only people actually walking on Walworth Ave. were gardeners and local workmen who had no interest in striking up a conversation with a neurotic lonely woman. They probably thought the coffee mug I was holding had a couple of fingers of Scotch in it.

The moms were usually driving their minivans and station wagons and not slowing down to introduce themselves. This is when I got the brilliant idea to join a country club. I figured I could rationalize it as a way to do business and give my family a place to go on summer weekends. Actors could come for a day of tennis or golf, and it could be a new tradition at my office for morale boosting outings. Brendan agreed it could be fun, and I started to do research.

I wanted a club that was nearby and family oriented. The perfect place was the Scarsdale Golf Club, walking distance from our house. It resembled Tara from *Gone with the Wind*, and I already fantasized myself going there for a gala in a velvet gown with opera gloves. There were a few details that made this club an odd choice. The glaring issue was the fact that a woman had never been accepted as the main family member requesting to join. It was always men, and their wives went along for the ride. This was obviously ludicrous, and that made me want to be accepted even more.

Their tradition was if a couple got divorced or the husband died, the woman was no longer a member. Whaaaaat? I knew my mission was to change that rule. (Okay, I'm not exactly Gloria Steinem or Emma Goldman, but we all need a hill to stand on.)

The second major issue was this particular club was not necessarily fond of Jews. I had been told that a few years back a debutante's escort was not welcome because he was Jewish. I remember, as a kid, my parents' outrage when they saw a sign at the Forest Hills racquet club that said no dogs or Jews allowed. This was the second reason I decided we were joining. Double down on everything that needed to change. I was going to have us accepted to a club that didn't want us. Well, to be fair, my Waspy husband would definitely be welcomed with a luau, but I was the one who needed to be accepted as the member and Brendan the spouse.

My parents were flabbergasted that I was so set on this acceptance. My mother would ask, "Why would you want to be around people that don't like you?" I loved a challenge, and I was not turning back. We needed to find a sponsor and then three letters of recommendation. You'd think I was running for public office, not a popularity contest with golf clubs. Luckily, one of my train ladies was a member via her husband. Martha was anxious for me to join so we could get more working women in the club. She also found members willing to write letters of recommendation, and the process began.

Honestly, I think the process moved ahead because, with Marx as my last name, the board thought I was part of a prominent Scarsdale family that owned Hasbro Toys. Let them think what they liked, even though I was way more Marx Brothers than part of a game and novelty dynasty.

After an arduous interview with a room full of bloated, waxy white dudes, I waited for their response. They had been confused as to why I found it important to be the joining member and not my husband, and I had explained that I wanted to bring business associates to the club as a business expense, which, to be fair, is exactly what these dudes had been doing since Roosevelt was in office. Somehow, that did the trick, and we were officially invited to be members of a club that honestly, in hindsight, seemed repugnant.

We've all heard the expression, "Be careful what you wish for," and in this case, I probably should have been more careful. Always up for a challenge, I plunged ahead and couldn't wait for the summer season to begin. Our kids loved going to the pool and summer day camp at the club, and while I never really felt at home, somehow I did my best to fit in. Riding on the high of being the first woman accepted as the family head of household might seem like a frivolous victory, but not to me. Baby steps are still steps.

When the girls were seven years old and Ryan was turning three, we tried to spend lots of time enjoying the privileges of membership. There were lots of barbecues and tennis tournaments, and I knew that I was giving my children something I never imagined for myself. Every year, the club had a big Mother's Day event. It was the start of the season, and I looked forward to enjoying this very idyllic pastime. My parents still couldn't understand how I could tolerate the other members, but that didn't stop me from trying to be a part of the hoi polloi.

My only real friends at the club were the two or three career-minded women, and unfortunately, that was a microcosm of the neighborhood back in the early '90s. Half the female population worked, and the other half played a lot of tennis and rushed to their aerobics classes. We resented the stay-at-home moms because, hey, they could stay home. They resented us for leaving every morning and doing stimulating work and earning our way to financial independence. I'm sure that rift still exists in suburban towns everywhere.

On this particular Mother's Day, unbeknownst to me, Kira and Lindsey signed me up for a mother/daughter swim relay race. It's a funny thing having children. They think their parents are capable of way more than they actually are. It's adorable, but sometimes it can be a hazard. Like on this particular day when there was an expectation that I would dive into a body of water and race to the other end of an Olympic-sized pool.

I am quite sure I had previously told them I couldn't swim, but somehow, they must have thought I was joking.

My entire childhood was a constant stream of things that could kill me. For instance, my mother told me to *never* let a pigeon shit on my head. Toxins will go straight to my brain. For years, you could see me weaving and bobbing away from anything that had wings. Then there was the concrete pavement. "Don't run!" she'd shout. "You'll crack your head open!" I had a distinct image of being a live Humpty Dumpty with an open skull. Last but not least was never go in the water after you've eaten. "You'll drop like a stone!" Rickets if I didn't drink my milk and rubella if I swallowed a paint chip. Who did this woman think she was raising? A hooligan?

Whenever we went to a pool, we just walked down the steps, threw a bit of water on ourselves, and then climbed back on a lounge chair and read our Harold Robbins novels. The very notion that I was jumping, certainly not diving, was preposterous.

The lifeguard blew his whistle, and I watched Kate and Cricket gracefully dive into the pool. The only way I could possibly get in the water was to slide in and throw myself toward a buoy. I could feel my back scraping against the deep end as I dog paddled to the safety of the rope. Basically, I looked like a sea otter flopping around, looking for sardines. I straddled the rope separating the racing lanes and saw my expectant little idiots waiting for me to reach them so they could swim back. It took a lot of lunging and dog paddling until I finally got close. I tried not to look to my left or the right. "Just worry about yourself," I kept mumbling.

At this point all of the other daughters had made their way to the deep end. Finally, I reached Kira and Lindsey, and I saw giddy admiration because their mom made it without needing to be resuscitated. They gleefully jumped in and swam, in spite of the obvious fact the race was over.

All the women in their Lily Pulitzer shifts and the men in their lime-green golf pants drinking their gin and tonics were not going to stop my fabulous Marx twins from finishing their race. These little beauties taught me a valuable lesson that day. Maybe joining a country club wasn't just my shallow end of a pool triumph, but a lesson in perseverance. I had exposed my kids to things that I was too afraid to try, and they were going to be fierce. I knew that I could change my family's narrative. Take chances, do the absurd. What did we have to lose? After my divorce, I found no solace in staying at a country club that certainly was not a good fit. I gave up my membership, and Brendan joined on his own. The extra cool thing about Brendan? Many years after our divorce, he became a marathon runner and even participated in an Ironman race. All of our kids had the opportunity to cheer an actual hero. At least one of their parents blessed them with athletic genes.

MEET-CUTE

I HAVE ALWAYS BEEN UP FOR A DARE. THE first one that I can remember was when my cousin, Wayne, dared me to chew on some aluminum foil. Apparently, if you have fillings, this act of derring-do is very uncomfortable. But like any good pool shark, I had a pristine set of ten-year-old chompers, and I was more than happy to stuff that Reynolds Wrap in my mouth. The look on my cousin's face was worth any possible side effects from chewing that foil.

Part of my soul is pure punk-ass bitch. Just try and tell me I can't do something and I will climb, jump and eat the dangerous challenge for breakfast. So I'm sure it will come as no surprise when my almost ex-husband told me, "Nobody's happy. Why do you think you should be happy? Who is gonna want to date a forty-two-year-old suburban mom with three young kids? *You* are no bargain." That was all the motivation I needed to make it my mission to prove him wrong.

It took a while to get my sea legs after we finally "uncoupled" (which frankly sounds like something that happens to train cars), but in my case it was the glorious freedom of having my own home and that I could coparent our kids and live with some peace and the knowledge I was doing the right thing. Getting a divorce was serious business, and I knew it was inevitable. It certainly was a tough time in the beginning, but sometimes doing the hard stuff is not that hard in retrospect. In the beginning, it felt like I was finally going away to college and living on my own, except for those three short people who required an endless supply of juice boxes and Hot Pockets.

After I finally got into a rhythm with our parenting schedule (one week on, one week off, except I was always parent-on-duty until dinnertime), I started to realize I could create a new social life, which is a euphemism for dating. My instructions to all my friends was specific. I told them I only wanted to date the kind of guy who was capable of running a small country or maybe find a cure for lactose intolerance. In other words, a prize package. I couldn't imagine dating someone who would be intimidated by my work ethic (being a boss lady) or not understand that my children always came first.

Surprisingly, without using dating sites (it was still only the late '90s and they weren't as prevalent as today), it seemed to be raining men. It's a timing strategy I suppose. Men in their late forties who were single were usually divorced guys who were not looking for a trophy wife just yet, just the opposite of what they already knew. They wanted someone who might have gently agreed to a settlement in a conference room with a mediator. The trophy wives came much later.

There were lawyers, a lovely guy in the Foreign Service, money managers, and a soupçon of business dudes. As nice as they all were, none of them felt like a future for my family. It was also messy when your new relationship has a few of their own kids because *The Brady Bunch* is just a fantasy with a cheesy laugh track.

One of my closest friends told me she had the perfect match but was waiting for the right time to introduce us because he had just ended his second marriage. I thought, *Oy vey, this might not be so perfect.* I trusted Shelley and her recommendation because she was whip smart and funny and knew exactly what I was searching for. She said, "Sandi, he's good looking, tall, a dentist, and . . . drum roll . . . no children." Apparently his first wife tragically died at a young age and his second marriage was short.

This was like winning a trifecta in the mature dating pool. A tall, good-looking, Jewish dentist with zero baggage! Oh God, please let us like each other.

It took a while for Mr. Magic to call me because he was a bit of a disorganized mess. His dental practice was extremely busy, and he seemed to be a bit forgetful when it came to fulfilling social obligations. Let's face it, he, like many other guys, needed a wife to do all the after-hours heavy lifting. Finally, with a bit of a nudge from Shelley, he called, and I still can remember saying, "Finally, you called! Are you supposed to be my Prince Charming?"

Pretty brazen coming from a woman who, according to my ex, was no bargain.

Keith laughed, and that definitely broke any awkward tension. Our first date was at a great burger joint near his Gramercy Park office called Pete's Tavern. The plan was to meet there at 7:00 p.m. I arrived a bit early, and when I went inside, I was hit with a tsunami of cigarette smoke and immediately went back outside. There was no way I could eat in there. This was a few years before Mayor Bloomberg banned indoor smoking.

After waiting outside in the cold (it was late January), I noticed a short woman in a dental hygienist costume running in my direction. "Are you Sandi? Keith wanted to let you know he's running late. Would you like to wait in his office?" This was before we were all attached to our cell phones, so communications were creative in these situations. I was more than happy to follow her to his office and was kind of impressed that he sent a foot soldier to find me.

As soon as I walked inside, I surveyed the situation. I immediately noticed two women in his waiting area holding boxes of baked goods. I guess I wasn't the only single lady vying for the attention of a single, professional guy with good posture. Keith was the equivalent of that one upright dude at a nursing home who still has his drivers' license: a catch. Even his office manager seemed to have her eye on the prize despite being happily married.

Keith poked his head out of his office, and I was immediately smitten. He had the biggest blue eyes and a kind face. In his soft-spoken manner, he told me he'd be done soon and he profusely apologized. This was when those gift laden women shot me with that look that could kill. I was an interloper with good teeth who was stealing their potential future husband.

A half hour later, after Keith politely accepted the quiche and apple pie respectively, we were out the door. I explained the smoke situation at Pete's, and he recommended we go to a great organic restaurant around the corner. I was impressed because back then, organic was more of a west coast vibe and this spot, Friend of a Farmer, was an anomaly.

We were both a bit nervous when we sat down, but I slowly relaxed, realizing I was sitting across from a lovely guy who was an extremely good listener. He ordered the pasta primavera, and I think (I'm not proud of this) I had a small salad. It was a nasty, first-date habit where I only ordered petite food on first dates so my partner would think I was not a glutton. So stupid, but I couldn't help myself.

While we chatted, I started to do the thing that I know many women do. I began a visual scan of Keith. I started at his hair, which at the time was sparse like the cartoon character Doug. I thought, *I'll get that head shaved bald*. Next were his glasses. They were very 1985 Bill Gates. *No problem, we will go optical shopping*. Next came his clothes, which gave "college senior with too much student debt" vibes. *Banana Republic, here we come*. Oh, and I forgot to mention he wore a denim jacket with the New York skyline sewn into the back. That would need to go to the Salvation Army. Why some of us feel the need to do a full *Queer Eye* episode on our men is beyond understanding, but we do.

Next, while I was cutting my olives and cucumbers into tiny bite-sized pieces like Princess Grace, I noticed that sweet and obviously hungry Keith was scarfing his creamy pasta with the fervor of a man just released from Sing Sing. I thought, *Jeez, I could have ordered anything and not worried about my table manners 'cause this guy eats like a potbellied pig.* I immediately started to relax and enjoy the rest of our dinner. After spending so many tense nights being told to sit up, keep elbows off the table, and put your damn napkin in your lap, I was being liberated by another barn animal. He was going to be my prince after all.

We left the restaurant, and I brazenly kissed him first before he put me in a cab. I knew he was the one. By our fourth date, with his shaved head and new glasses, it became obvious to his staff (and all those wistful patients) that Keith had met his match. Maybe I *was* a bargain. And just maybe it is possible to fall in love after forty, with three kids in the suburbs, and truly be happy.

Never let anyone tell you that you don't deserve to be happy. I found a partner that had enough of a sturdy ego to allow me to be myself, even if it meant having to give away his favorite jacket and his ill-fitting Dockers. Nobody had to dare me to spend my life with this wonderful man, and twenty-five years later, I'm still realizing that being in the right relationship is a lovely thing. He still shovels his food, and now I do too.

WIND BENEATH MY WINGS

A TRIP TO OUR LOCAL MALL WAS HAIR RAISING, not only because we couldn't afford to actually buy anything at Macy's or Dressbarn (which we couldn't), but because Greta, God bless her, could not contain herself when her favorite music was blasting on the store's speakers. And to add to the level of embarrassment these trips caused, I might add that, on more than one occasion, we watched as store clerks cut up her credit card while we stood at the register because it apparently was on the "Bad Credit" list. Nothing like being a shy eight-year-old walking a few paces behind a woman belting out "What's New Pussycat" along with Welsh heart-throb, Tom Jones, at full volume.

And then there were those trips to the grocery store where she would sing along with Peggy Lee while pushing her cart—her eyes closed in some kind of kinship reverie, "If that's all there is my friends / Then let's keep dancing." Growing up as Greta's daughter was your basic "choose your own adventure." I knew from a fairly young age that raising us kids thwarted her desire to be a lounge singer. She loved to remind us about those weddings and parties where she had been hired to entertain the guests. Once a year, while Rhonda and I would watch our previously mentioned absolute favorite movie, *The Wizard of Oz*, our mom always knew exactly when to come in our room and join Judy Garland when she sang "Over the Rainbow." Disconcerting, but we knew to keep our traps shut unless we wanted to suffer the wrath of a woman disrespected and insulted.

She was the queen of the silent treatment and had cornered the market on Jewish guilt. A master class in manipulation kept us from making any rude comments or being critical of her falsetto. Of course, all my friends loved her because she was the warm wacky mom who was generous with her affection to a fault. If she had been around during the social media era, I shudder to think of all those posts she'd have put on my friends' pages.

But Greta also suffered greatly from an unlucky hand our family had been dealt. Being broke is miserable, but also having your oldest child in and out of the hospital because of her leaky heart is an unimaginable burden. It didn't help that my dad couldn't hold onto a job or that their constant fighting made my sister and me duck and cover. She was the family glue, and it seemed, at any time, it would all become unstuck.

Somehow, she managed to keep her head held high and did what was necessary to put food on the table. Her pride, being one of the top saleswomen in the Bloomingdale's baby department, was unparalleled. She loved to read us thank-you notes from her customers and I like to think I inherited that gift. The ability to sell ice to a snowman.

Unfortunately, her positive veneer came to a crashing nosedive when my sister suddenly died on July 3, 1974. My mother never recovered from her grief. How could she? As the mother of my own three kids, I can't imagine surviving that level of despair. She wore an expression of utter defeat, and when she decided it was time to retire, my parents packed up their cluttered apartment and shipped everything to their new home in Sunrise, Florida.

There was definitely a small part of her that thought, *If my only child* (that would be me), *doesn't have enough time to spend with me, I'll show her and move far away.* Punish me with a dollop of guilt on the side. Irrational reasoning for sure, but I knew that move was inevitable.

They settled in quickly and made lots of friends in their new lifestyle. Phase One at Sunrise Lakes became their paradise. One day my mom called and in excitement told me she was going to be a soloist with the Sunrise Serenaders, a choral group that "gigged" all over southern Florida. Finally, at seventy, she could restart her career. My dad was almost as excited as she was.

Everyone in the group wore white slacks and Hawaiian shirts, and they toured all the local con-dominium clubhouses and nursing homes on the weekends. Nobody worked, so technically they could have been booked on a Tuesday at noon, but maybe they thought if they performed on weekends, their kids and their grandchildren could be in the audience. My mother invested in a Mr. Microphone to practice her big closing number, "Wind Beneath My Wings." Keeping it real, I kept thinking that this was a wildly optimistic choice of song because, as much as I knew my mom would give it her all, she wasn't exactly Bette Midler. But then I also thought, well, singing at local nursing homes could be a confidence booster because the audience was 90 percent around ninety years old and 100 percent partially deaf. Every week, she'd call and report back about how each appearance went. She loved to tell me how she "killed," which could have been entirely possible based on their audience's demographic.

After she gained enough confidence with the Serenaders, Greta decided it was time to throw my dad a surprise birthday party and hire the organist to accompany her while, in front of family and friends, she sang "Wind Beneath My Wings" during dessert at a local eatery. We all flew down to spend a few days with them and help celebrate my dad's birthday. Frankly, I was surprised at this point they were still married because my mom assured me from a very young age that they were getting a divorce. Somehow, fifty years later, they seemed to finally be happy, sort of.

Arnold knew how to keep her happy by just adoring her without question and also aiding and abetting her poor dietary choices. As an insulin dependent diabetic, you'd think those peaches in cling syrup would not be her healthiest of snacks, but she just gamed the system by adjusting her insulin. I knew this was not a healthy lifestyle, but I couldn't insulate her from her subconscious death wish.

We all arrived for the big celebration, and I instructed our kids (who were still quite young) to clap wildly for their grandma when she sang and not to talk or giggle as she reached for that mic. The party was held in an eatery at a strip mall that was flanked by a kidney dialysis center and a podiatrist. (Hey, it was Florida.) There was a neon sign above the restaurant that flickered on and off, Chops and Cocktails. Inside, there were thirty or so local friends and relatives.

My dad appeared shocked when he walked in, but I think he was giving an Oscar-level performance. Everyone loved the food and cocktails, and just before dessert, my mom came rushing over to me, wild-eyed and sweating, and whispered, "I left Mr. Microphone at home!" I offered to drive back and get it, but she thought people would start to leave if she didn't sing soon. I encouraged her to sing without the mic considering the room was fairly small, but she had a better idea. This blousy, beautiful broad picked up an empty crystal wine glass and decided *that* would be her mic. The organist, sitting behind his Casio keyboard, started to play, and my mother sang into that goblet like Bette herself. She even moved it away from her mouth to prevent some sort of imaginary feedback.

I was absolutely gobsmacked. Not because of her quick thinking but because of her gorgeous voice. As an adult, I could let go of my childhood embarrassment and actually listen to her sing—and boy could she sing. It was pitch perfect and with so much heart, I started to cry. My heart was breaking for her because she never had a chance to fulfill her dream and use her talent until now. I suppose late is better than never, but it still made me sad. I realized that day that I needed to also find my voice—not as a singer, but as a writer and performer.

Unfortunately, that was the last time my mother could sing because she had a stroke the following year. All those refined-sugar shenanigans finally caught up to her. Shortly thereafter she was gone, and I was furious at my dad for letting it happen. Maybe it wasn't logical, but that's what I believed.

My dad flew to New York on JetBlue with my mom in cargo as we prepared for her burial. We remained nonpracticing Jews without a temple, so once again we needed Angie's List to find a rabbi. I decided not to take any chances with our rental officiant not properly honoring Greta, so I chose to give her eulogy and to really honor this fabulous woman. I'd bring a big CD player and blast her big song after I spoke. I had cued up "Wind

Beneath my Wings" on Bette's greatest hits album and perched the player on the edge of the stage. I spoke to the congregation and reminded them of all the magic my mother created in spite of a painful and tragic life. How she loved big and cared deeply for her family and friends.

When I was done, I pressed play and let Bette wash over the synagogue. I sat in a seat right in front of the CD player and suddenly realized that if I didn't hit stop at the exact right moment, the next song would begin. I could hear crying all around me, and I knew I had to focus. And then it happened. "The Boogie Woogie Bugle Boy" started to play, and everyone started to laugh. I was so embarrassed at first, but then I thought, *Good job, Sandi*. I had captured the essence of Greta Handelman. Loud, messy, complicated, and joyful. Somehow, I'd like to believe she was there with us that day—and was proud of me and finally found a little joy.

Sammy's Roumanian

I SAT AT A LONG, CROWDED TABLE AT THE popular and quote famous restaurant Sammy's Roumanian. Across from me was my dad, Arnold, and sitting to my left, holding my hand, was my husband, Keith. An untrained eye would have seen a happy family gathering taking place on a Sunday evening. What the rest of the dining patrons didn't know was that Keith was holding my hand because he was concerned there was a high probability that I'd grab my fork and try to stab my dad. I wish his concerns were unfounded, but unfortunately, he would be correct. The rage I felt for this man was big and blind. It was perhaps unwarranted, but at that moment, it seemed like a completely reasonable feeling. I need to explain this anger.

My parents were married for fifty years. For as long as I can remember, my mother had told me, in her conspiratorial tone, "I'm leaving your father." This was not the case (as mentioned), and I suppose thinking he could be out the door any minute didn't exactly lead my sister and I to do any daddy-daughter bonding.

My father could not keep a job, and the level of dissatisfaction my mother felt seemed to grow exponentially as I got older. The crazy and truly sad part of this story was that my dad always adored my mother. He loved telling us when we were kids that when he met my mom, she was built like a brick shithouse. That's right. He described my mother as a brick shithouse. It was apparently a compliment?

The only way he could stay in my mom's good graces was to enable her to eat all of her favorite sugary treats. This may sound, no pun intended, sweet, but the woman was a diabetic, and his insistence in wooing her with Jell-O and Pop-Tarts was not helping my mother maintain her insulin levels. No matter how often I begged her to change her diet, it fell on two sets of deaf ears.

After they chose to leave New York and retire in a Florida community called Sunrise, the risky behavior became untenable. My sweet mother, Greta, who I adored, eventually died after falling into a two-week diabetic coma. I suspect if a Dexter-style forensic expert surveyed their condo, the murder weapon, a cheesecake-dirty fork, would have been in the sink. From that moment forward, all I could think about was how my father was responsible for my mother's death. I loved this woman with my whole heart. She had a lifetime of heartache, burying her oldest child, never fulfilling her true potential as a businesswoman, and having a life partner that drove her bananas, and she was gone.

My dad was lost without her, and I know I should have been more sympathetic, but my anger consumed me. A year after her death, it was time for my dad to fly to New York so we could have my mother's unveiling. It's a Jewish tradition where a year after you bury a loved one, the etched tombstone is unveiled. A cotton cloth is laid atop it, and after a rabbi says a few words, abracadabra! He whips off the cloth. It's the saddest magic trick ever created.

A couple of days before the unveiling, I picked him up from the JetBlue terminal and drove him back to our home in Scarsdale. He seemed smaller and frail. Living without his partner had taken a toll. I tried to make small talk, but he just wanted to listen to a Yankee game on the radio. Just as well, I supposed. I couldn't bait him into an argument while he was engaged in who was pitching and hitting in the Bronx.

I had promised him that after the unveiling, before he had to return home, I'd take him to his favorite restaurant, Sammy's, on the Lower East Side. It had been an institution since the Nixon administration—or maybe earlier. It was always a mess, with dirty windows and a small foyer with business cards tacked everywhere. The tables were all shoved together, each one with an old-fashioned seltzer bottle and a small tub of chicken fat (also known as schmaltz). The waiters were all over seventy years old, and I suspected they had worked these tables since their own bar mitzvahs. Their white shirts were splotchy with what was probably that table fat, and they didn't ask you what you wanted as much as demanded you order the flank steak and potatoes.

The size of each portion could have fed a family of five. The coup de grâce was the bottomless vodka that was poured as soon as we took a sip. This was actually the first time bottle service was in use.

In addition to all the meats and starches, there was entertainment. This was the highlight of the Sammy's experience. A Casio keyboard was set up in the middle of the room, and a middle-aged dude, also in a white rumpled shirt and sporting an unwieldy toupee, took requests for songs from his favorite singers like Sinatra and Billy Joel. His most popular request? "Piano Man." He changed the lyrics so he sang, "Give us a song, I'm the schmata man!" Oy vey.

All of the restaurant's patrons would join in the sing-along. Coachella and Bonaroo have nothing on this wild crowd, singing and banging their silverware. The vodka was the only thing that kept me somewhat calm. I am not really a drinker of hard alcohol. I love wine, but I'm also a cheap date.

Perhaps, weighing under a hundred pounds doesn't leave much room for absorption.

On this occasion, I was drinking my weight in spirits. By the time the check arrived, I was starting to feel queasy and unsteady on my feet. Keith paid our waiter and slowly got me and my dad to the front door. Even after we walked outside, I could hear the entertainer bellowing, "New York, New York!" Our car was parked across the street, and Keith stuck me in the back seat and managed to stuff my father in the front, riding shotgun.

Before we could leave, I suddenly felt extremely ill. I opened the back door and left the contents of my dinner and perhaps some angry bile on Christie Street. During this exorcism, my dad, clueless, asked Keith about his favorite baseball players. Keith figured he'd humor my dad and patiently wait for me to finish leaving the contents of my stomach on the curb. When I gave him the thumbs up, we left the detritus behind us. It was a long drive home. I opened my window and hung my head out like a golden retriever, sniffing the cool air and looking for a horizon to calm my nausea.

Finally, we arrived home. Keith carefully helped my dad, who was also a bit unsteady, inside. I ventured inside and wandered toward our bedroom. Keith understood how important it was that we got my father ready for his return flight the next morning, so he went into his room, made sure he was packed, and set an alarm. *God help us if he misses the flight*, was all I could think.

After my dad was settled in, Keith came upstairs to our room and couldn't find me. He checked the bed, the bathroom; I was missing. His first thought was perhaps I had wandered in the kitchen. Nope. He proceeded to run outside, worried that in my current state of rage and vodka-infused confusion, I could have wandered into traffic. Nope, not outside. I was passed out in our walk-in closet, cradling one leather boot. I have no idea why or how, but those are the facts.

This angel of a husband somehow managed to scrape me up, wash me, and stuff me into bed. It was important that I, too, get a good night's sleep to get my dad back to that airport. Teamwork was in full force.

The next morning, I awoke with a start and despite feeling the effects of the bacchanal the night before, I was up and motivated to get Arnold home. We still hadn't addressed the issue of my hostility, but in retrospect, I'm fairly certain he knew. I got him in our car, loaded his luggage, and headed to JFK Airport. We made small talk heading out into the highway traffic, and I just kept thinking to myself, *Be intentional.*

Finally, I pulled up to the JetBlue terminal and I did the unthinkable, I double-parked. Anyone who has ever attempted this maneuver at a New York airport knows this will lead to a harsh confrontation with a traffic officer or worse, but in that moment I didn't care. I got out, helped my dad with his bag, and before he could walk inside his terminal, I grabbed him tight in a hug. Startled, he initially pulled away, but I said in a very low voice, "I love you, Dad." He didn't respond, and I was okay with that, because it was at that moment, I could finally let go. Forgive him. He did his best.

Bad Timing

THE PHONE RANG IN OUR NOW BROOM-SWEPT empty house. We were lucky enough to sell in what was considered a terrible housing market (2007), and like that famous IKEA commercial, it felt like we had really gotten away with something. I imagined myself shouting, "Start the car! Start the car!"

The only sign of life left in our kitchen, besides the hum of our appliances, was a landline ringing. That now-obsolete invention, a phone attached to a wall, kept ringing away until I decided (in spite of my assumption that it was a telemarketer trying to sell me a home alarm system) to answer. It was not a sales pitch but instead a nurse calling from the Sunrise nursing home, which by no coincidence was also my dad's home and had been for the past six months.

In my experience, this was the kind of call you get at three in the morning, not at lunchtime, but death is not usually scheduled, and apparently my dad was gone.

Standing stock still, I was not necessarily shocked (he had not been doing well for a while), but it's never easy to hear this kind of news. Officially an orphan, I had to figure out what to do next. There was an idling van outside our door, filled to the brim with all of our furniture, clothes, and the mementos of our messy but happy life at 1070 Post Road, waiting to drive to our next life's adventure in White Plains. Yikes. How would I plan a funeral, get my dad "mailed" to New York via JetBlue, and help our family move all on this one hot August day?

Oh, and it also happened to be my birthday.

I couldn't even find my address book with all our relatives and family friends to call and help plan. Thank God my one local cousin, Walter, came to my rescue and alerted everyone. We somehow managed to get the move in motion while I called all the appropriate people in Florida to expedite. Apparently, my parents, who never had the ability to plan for their financial future, *did* plan for their deaths. They even prepaid their air freight and coffin fees. God bless them for that. Instead of a service at a chapel, we once again rented a rabbi to meet the family at the cemetery, Mount Hebron, where we all stood in inappropriate funeral attire: shirts and shorts in dark colors—hey, moving is hard and boxes were yet to be unpacked, so no judgment.

After we left the cemetery, we had a small memorial lunch at our local diner, and I ordered (in honor of Arnold, the gourmand) scrambled eggs and bacon with ketchup. It was delicious, and it made me remember what my life with this man was like: confusing, infuriating, and often frustrating. But he was my only dad.

The Beat Went On

IT WAS A GORGEOUS SPRING AFTERNOON, and Keith and I decided to go for a leisurely stroll in Soho. It was one of those days when what seemed like every other New Yorker had the same idea. After a long winter, we could finally saunter without worrying about icy rain or freezing toes. West Broadway was so crowded that to get from one end of the street to the other, we had to basically play Frogger, working our way through the obstacles (which in this case were tourists who did not understand the rules of the road: eyes forward and walk at a brisk pace).

And that's when I saw him. Jack, who had been my very first love, walking toward us with his partner. We both made eye contact, so a successful duck was not going to be an option. That awkward moment was upon us, and I did that thing many of us do when we see someone and can't decide if it's a warm embrace or just a stop and chat. I'm pretty touchy feely, so it was a big hug, but the kind where you don't get too close whilst hugging, just sort of square dancing so our body parts wouldn't actually touch. Then came the catching up, which was certainly the CliffsNotes version since we hadn't seen each other up close in forty years. I was flattered that after all those years he recognized me, but perhaps it's because of my deep devotion to good skin care and hair products.

Then Jack told me he's now Jake. Why give up a consonant for a vowel? I was confused. Apparently, he was now touring with his one-man show called, "A Jew Grows in Brooklyn"—and when he told me, I made that rookie mistake by telling him "Oh, I know!" Busted. I hadn't been stalking him on Facebook, but I *had* seen his show's poster slapped on the side of our local Scarsdale Jewish Center. Somehow, my first boyfriend had become a star of Yiddish theater. After a bit more awkward chatter and the offer of free tickets to his show, we said our good-byes.

So, who was this guy and how did we meet, you ask?

I had just returned from a week's vacation at Club Med. As soon as I returned from this gleeful bacchanal, I knew I wanted to show off my newly bronzed body at my favorite disco/dance hall. I asked my roommate to join me, but she was exhausted from a trying week at work. I was not to be deterred, so I put on my new favorite outfit and piled on the eye and lip rouge for maximum hotness. To be specific, I was wearing a rawhide halter top covered in feathers and beads. I looked like Cher during her "Half-Breed" platinum album phase. I had on way too much black eyeliner, and my hair was what we used to call Bridge and Tunnel. In other words, full Queens tacky. I looked like a Saturday Night fever dream.

I decided to go to a place called The Red Parrot. It was a huge disco on West Fifty-Seventh Street and Tenth Avenue that also featured big band music. In other words, it was a slice of heaven. As soon as I walked in, I was hit with a wall of smoke and men's cologne. The band was playing Duke Ellington, and everyone was vibing to it as if they were listening to Donna Summer. Hey, it was 1982, and swing wasn't exactly the most requested music at clubs, except at The Red Parrot. I felt like I was home in the very best possible way, except for the smoke and Aramis wafting around my face.

Then I spotted the drummer doing a solo, and I thought, *I am going to try and charm the pants off this sexy, intense guy with gnarled drummer fingers and a beautiful face.* He had big brown peepers and curly, unkempt hair in a black suit that appeared to have traveled more than a few miles between dry cleanings.

I needed a plan. How was I going to get his attention? I knew that the band would get a break and I was going to stalk him if necessary. Who wouldn't want to be stalked by a tan, tiny girl with big hair in a leather halter?

Right before their break, I scurried into a densely populated bathroom where girls were doing lines of coke off of their tiny compact mirrors and the dirty bathroom surfaces. No one was considering germs or whether they were inhaling any carcinogens; it was a crazy and optimistic era before there were actual consequences, like AIDS, to slow us down. I checked my sweaty face, made a few minor repairs, and with my eye on the prize, I headed to the bar in search of the drummer.

I ordered a gin and tonic and thought about this sexy musician and how the only drummer I knew was Alan Potashnick, who could skillfully drum "Wipeout" on his steering wheel. I felt a tap on my shoulder, and when I turned around, I saw *him*. "Hi, I'm Jack. You were really grooving to the music!"

Tongue-tied, I still managed to respond, "Yes! I used to be a dancer, and I just loved your drum solo!" Oh God, just thinking about it now makes me cringe, but back then it was my truth. Jack then told me that drummers get along great with dancers because we both have *rhythm!* Maybe it was a cheesy pickup line—and I was all in.

Jack asked if I'd stick around until he was done with his last set and then we could hang out. I enthusiastically nodded my head and could not believe that I was going to nail the drummer. I had observed all the women vying for his attention, but he picked *me*. His last set included his big solo, "Sing Sing Sing," and I was ready ready ready to go home with him. And that's exactly what I did.

We took a cab to his fourth floor walkup on McDougal Street in the village, and I quickly looked around for signs that he wasn't a crazy murderer. I know, it seems like I was already putting myself at risk, but when I saw all his family photos and stacks of sheet music, I knew I was in good hands. Jack also had a very old rescue hound that he had to carry those four flights every day, so that was proof positive: Jack was an angel. This was more than a one-night stand, and I loved climbing up his ladder into his loft bed and feeling very lucky—maybe a bit winded after those four flights, but at twenty-five (in reasonably good shape), I was not complaining.

At some point during this wild affair, Jack mentioned he had a girlfriend but they were taking a break, which I have since learned means "I might be cheating on my girlfriend." I was clueless or I would definitely have followed girl code and not have seduced him if I had known . . . I think? Who knows. Also, it was hard to not fall in love with a guy whose parents were Holocaust survivors.

After a couple of months, in spite of my fantasy that I would become his Penny Lane (sitting in the back of his tour bus), the inevitable occurred. In the kindest of breakups ever, he told me he and his girlfriend had reconciled.

I stewed in my misery for a few days before I shook it off and started dating, never wearing that leather halter again because it just felt like it belonged to a very specific time.

Seeing Jack/Jake now was really special and made me a bit nostalgic for an era that seemed almost imaginary. It was a complete coincidence that my first grandson is named Jack. Perhaps one day he too will become a drummer and change his name to Jake.

Just Say Neigh

VACATIONING WITH TWO TWEENS CAN BE daunting. I've always prided myself as a "half-full glass of blind faith" and exotic travel was a perfect place for my misguided optimism. I had scrolled the internet and found a website with colorful trips designed for the whole family. Being an aspirational adventurer, I decided white water rafting and zip-lining in Costa Rica was a wonderful experience for two thirteen-year-olds, and their mom and stepdad. Ryan was at summer camp having his own adventure, and I thought, *This is the summer of saying yes to things I hadn't imagined I'd ever accomplish on my own or with my girls.*

The only research done was staring at gorgeous families with toned arms and legs on the travel and tourism website. That was all the evidence needed for me to mindlessly enter my credit card information and book a trip without consulting Keith, who, it must be noted, is an incredibly good sport.

I had recovered from my early years of toddler travel and felt emboldened by the twins' independence and ability to adapt to most situations. This was going to be the adventure of a lifetime. Everyone was excited and the flight was smooth, except for the odd choice of showing the film *A River Wild*, a movie about a raft being held hostage with Meryl Streep and her family menaced by Kevin Bacon and his sidekick. Terrifying, but at that time in air travel, there were limited options for entertainment, so we watched.

After a two-hour drive to our hotel in Manuel Antonio Park, we settled in and were in awe at all the local fauna and flora. The kids were captivated by the local sloths very slowly climbing a tree and a butterfly museum a few feet from our resort. Clearly, my impetuous travel lust made for a great choice for a memorable week of adventure. We all went zip-lining in the rain forest, and I was actually brave enough to follow my brood and literally zip through the tree line like Spider-Man, whooping and laughing like a hyena the whole ride. We all were giddy and impressed with our collective derring-do.

The next day was the main event: white water rafting with a guide. I somehow forgot to read the small print and did not realize this would be grade four rapids, considered dangerous and perhaps not ideal for youngish children. As we were driven to the rafting site, I became increasingly nervous. I had made it my goal to expose our kids to these kinds of adventures, because I was raised in a big worry bubble by Greta, who feared the worst-case scenario was around every corner. I could be kidnapped or drown at a moment's notice. Of course, we didn't have any money to motivate a kidnapping or live near a body of water, but this did not stop Greta's relentless neurosis.

My kids would be brave and flexible in all situations. I kept my worry to myself and figured we would be fine and our life vests and guide would keep us safe. As soon as we arrived at the charter hut, we were introduced to our guide and our fellow travelers. I started to do an approximate weight count. My two kids' combined weight was around 140 pounds, Keith and I, another 260. I was already thinking, *That seems like a lot for one rubber raft.* Even though our fellow travelers did not have kids, they were both fairly large, and I started thinking there was no way we would stay afloat. Our guide did not share my concern, and he instructed all of us to put on our vests and these small helmets that in my opinion would not save us from any sort of catastrophic capsize.

My two dopey adventurers scampered into their seats, no fear, just excitement. Keith and I stepped in much more gingerly and took our assigned seats. The guide knew well enough to be sizing us up, deciding who would get oars and who (me) would just sit and keep an eye on our family. As soon as we pushed off from shore, my fear could not be hidden. The water turned white almost immediately, and at that moment, I remembered that I couldn't swim.

That life jacket offered little in the way of comfort, but I was not going to let my fear become contagious, so I just sat quietly and held on as tight as I could without puncturing the raft. Within a few minutes, the big male German tourist flew out of the raft and swam toward a sharp and slimy rock. I knew he was German because this 200-pound dude was crying in German. My family looked only mildly concerned—while I thought I was going overboard next.

I will admit (and I'm not proud of this admission), listening to his plea in German did not instill a level of empathy at that moment because, hey, I'm a post-war Jewess.

A moment of distress coming from the Costa Rican "drink" somehow felt like a karmic event. The poor guy was obviously waaaay too young to have participated in the Holocaust, but I wasn't exactly thinking rationally. The raft made a wide turn and fetched the waterlogged dude and we continued.

I was ready to quit and started begging the guide to let me off the boat. I whined, "Pleeeease! Let me go. Just me! My family can stay. I can't do this!" I was ready to sell my family down the river, literally. The guide laughed and told me to sit back down and if I didn't quit, I could have an extra bag of cookies and a Capri Sun. I had instantaneously become a toddler. So much for setting an example of bravery and sportsmanship. If my daughters could have pretended that I wasn't their mom, they would have at that point.

Somehow, I suppose thinking about those sugar cookies, I stayed the course and none of my fellow travelers took a header out of that raft and we safely made it to shore.

I could not stop shaking the rest of the day but took pleasure in how excited everyone else was reflecting upon their collective bravery. The rest of the trip was lovely and calm, mostly hanging out on a quiet beach and eating tasty local food. We did it!

And though I had no regrets, I decided our next family vacation would be a bit more docile. I found a resort in New York (so we could save on air fare) and an easy drive to New Paltz. The hotel was called the Mohonk Mountain House, and it was a huge Victorian building situated next to a lovely man-made lake and a place to go rock scrambling.

There were also colorful rocking chairs set on their huge covered porch. My kind of vacation was waiting. I knew nothing bad could happen in this serenity, and I was proud of myself for finding this gem.

We booked two rooms (one for us and Ryan, and the other for our now sixteen-year-old twins) and settled in. Everything at the hotel looked like the original decor. The hotel was built in the 1800s, and I think they hadn't changed the wallpaper or rugs since they had apparently expanded years later. It distinctly reminded me of *The Shining*, which was punctuated by my identical twins standing in the hall waiting for us to go to the dining hall. Think "Red Rum, Red Rum."

The halls leading to their restaurant were lined with photos of distinguished guests from the last hundred years, all in sepia tones. I thought I might have seen a few pairs of eyes in those photos follow us into the dining hall. These were not like those celebrity photos at our local dry cleaner.

Entering this mess hall, I was hit with the scent of egg salad and BenGay. I guess you could say the guests were mature. We acclimated to all the fun activities, and we all went on the "much calmer than Costa Rican" water and also did a bit of rock scrambling. Once again, I patted my own back for this wise holiday trip.

Keith then informed me he had booked us on a day of horseback riding. I pretended to be thrilled, but once again, my sheltered childhood hadn't prepared me for mounting a big, powerful animal. The next morning, we all clamored down to the dude ranch and were met by the local dude, who started bringing out horses for the five of us. I had requested the oldest most infirm of the group. The dude assured me my horse was slow and gentle. The rest of my family all crawled up on their horses, absolutely fearless, and I did feel a certain pride, knowing my plan to make them less nervous than their mom was working. All eyes on me, it was my turn to climb up onto my sweet old girl.

It was too high, and I suddenly got scared. Every member of the Marx/Marshall clan was cheering me on. "You can do it, Mom! Let's go!" Ughhh, I knew I couldn't bail on this, but I literally couldn't seem to reach the stirrups. And what I couldn't stop thinking about was Keith's first wife, who had died many years before we had met. You might wonder, how did Fran die? She fell off a horse. She was an expert at dressage and had an unfortunate freak accident on a rainy and muddy afternoon. It was reasonable for me to be anxious.

I knew Keith wouldn't take a chance losing a second wife, particularly in a similar situation, but, hey, it did make me slightly more neurotic.

The horse wrangler got a step ladder for me, and then there was no excuse or escape. Gingerly, I put one foot and then the next on the little stool and just as I was ready to throw myself on the saddle, the horse swooned and fainted. Just laid down on the ground with flies circling her head. I knew she wasn't dead because she winked at me. This gorgeous animal faked her own death so I wouldn't have to take her for an awkward ride. That wink said, "I've got you, girl. I don't want you on my back any more than you wanna be here." Everyone laughed because it seemed so crazy. This gentle lady slowly got back up, and I politely declined a second try. I was much happier waving at the gang and being in charge of photography instead. Every once in a while, an outsider like that sweet horse can create a divine intervention. As Mr. Rogers loved to say, "Look for the helpers."

You Got To Be In It To Win It

A SILLY STORY . . .

An advantage of living in an urban setting is that entertainment is always a short walk from home. Keith and I were lucky enough to have a cool apartment in White Plains, a New York suburb that had lots to offer in the way of movie theaters, restaurants, and shopping. On a cold Friday night, we decided to go for a later dinner at one of our favorite spots in a Ritz Carlton hotel, next to our building. Too lazy to research a new spot, we decided an evening of tapas and tequila was a perfect way to start the weekend. The Christmas holidays were around the corner, and we were feeling festive.

To access the restaurant, the hotel had a dedicated elevator that was basically a big glass tube. We would hold onto a hand rail and "whooosh" up the forty floors in what seemed like seconds. All of White Plains below. It was a bit terrifying but somehow sexy. The restaurant was packed, but we luckily got a table and enjoyed our baby octopus and lots of tapas. A pitcher of margaritas washed away all of our week's worries. Keith paid the check, and we meandered, stumbled really, back to that glass tube. I knew descending to the lobby would require my concentration in order to not get sick and leave my "small bites" on the elevator's glass in its partially digested form.

As soon as the doors closed, I looked down and, on the floor of the elevator cab, I saw something shiny. I picked it up and realized it was a scratch-off lottery ticket that had *not* been scratched. This was like seeing a holy shroud. I could practically hear angels humming around me. I have always believed I was a born winner. This was reinforced in the third grade when I was awarded Miss Posture and gifted a crown. I bested an entire class by having the ability to walk the perimeter of our health class with a book on my head longer than any other student. A year later, I won a raffle for an ice cream cake at Baskin Robbins. Obviously, I was destined to win lots of things, like lottery money. As a parent, I would sit on the middle school pickup line and kill time, scratching those lottery tickets. I'd be rubbing away and tiny gray cinders would be flying around the front seat. If one ticket garnered me five dollars, even though I had spent ten dollars in tickets, I'd take that as a victory. Math was never my strong suit.

But I knew that one day, I'd hit it big, and on this particular night, my Spidey sense was screaming, "This is your lucky day!" I drunkenly demanded Keith find a coin so I could start scratching this holiday-themed ticket. I had to match the ornamental balls to win $10,000. There were also reindeer and snowmen, but the idea was to get four balls. Even in my drunken stupor, I became hyper-focused as I started uncovering each square. I had to bravely keep one hand on the handrail so I wouldn't careen against one of those glass windows.

I stared at the ticket and I couldn't believe what I saw. Four balls and we had just won ten thousand dollars! Keith and I started jumping up and down in the elevator.

I could feel a slight skip and I thought, *Oh great, will we become a new line in an Alanis Morissette song, Ironic?* They won the big prize right before the elevator plunged them to their death.

Before we even got halfway down to the lobby, the money was spent. We decided we could finally take our family to Hawaii for their February school break. Having three kids had always prevented us from luxury travel that required expensive plane tickets, but now, we could go nuts! As soon as we got in the lobby, we showed our doorman our winning ticket. He was thrilled for us and probably thought that perhaps he'd get a better Christmas tip that year. We exited the hotel and, holding hands, started to skip home. Keith is six feet tall and I'm five feet two inches, so the sight of this odd drunk couple skipping home probably seemed a bit off kilter.

As soon as we got home, Keith scooped up Elvis, our little dog, to take him for a walk. He also took the lottery ticket and stuffed it in his coat pocket. At first I thought he was concerned I'd run away with our filthy lucre, but then I figured he wanted to savor the moment of our newfound fortune.

While they were gone, I opened my laptop and started rooting around various websites like Trivago, looking for the best travel packages. I wanted to surprise the kids, after I had everything worked out. Fifteen minutes later, Keith returned looking pale and upset. Immediately my imagination told me he was robbed and the ticket was gone. That was not the case. Keith pulled out the ticket and told me that he had read the small print, looking to see where we had to go to collect our winnings.

I had visions of getting dressed up in a fancy suit and being photographed holding one of those large cardboard checks at the lottery office. (As a side note, I fantasized winning the Publishers Clearing House prize for years. I used to look through the peephole of our apartment waiting for

Ed McMahon and the Prize Patrol to show up, with balloons and a television camera.)

Instead, Keith informed me that the fine print said the following, "If you think you really won, then go to the North Pole to collect your prize!" It was someone's idea of a practical joke. I was not laughing. In that moment, it felt like I lost ten thousand dollars of *my* money. It had slipped through our drunken, swollen fingers (too much Margarita salt). I was relieved I hadn't told our kids because they would have reminded us of this debacle for the rest of our lives.

Here's the thing, for a half hour, I was so happy and thrilled to be a winner. It's an undeniable feeling, and I'm sure most of us fantasize winning Powerball all the time. Part of the fun is the anticipation. Maybe my destiny is not to be a winner but remain a dreamer. As the New York State Lottery campaign always used to say, "All you need is a dollar and a dream."

A Hair Away From Greatness

IT WAS A TYPICAL SUNDAY AT OUR HOUSE. Keith and I tried to solve *The New York Times* crossword puzzle while I lazed around thinking about what we *should* have been doing, such as exploring a museum or taking our three extremely unwieldy dogs to the park. Then Keith's cell phone rang. I knew without hearing him speak it was a patient with an emergency.

You would assume my husband was an obstetrician or a cardiologist, but as I've bragged before, the man is a dentist. A very unusual dentist. He believes that no one should ever suffer from mouth pain if it can be avoided. He even makes house calls to the elderly, bringing his bag of tricks. I once witnessed him carrying a garbage bag filled with nitrous oxide for one of these emergencies. This man deserves a gold medal (which, not to be too disgusting, could be fashioned with just a few gold fillings).

When we married, his friends and family warned me I'd be a dentist widow. I thought the only cliché "widows" involved golf.

On this particular Sunday, Keith asked if I'd like to join him, going with him and his patient to his office. When he saw my confusion, he explained that I'd really want to meet this particular patient. I was intrigued. He then said, "It's Carole King." *The* Carole King. One of the most famous song-writers and award-winning singers of our generation. A woman celebrated at the Kennedy Center while Aretha Franklin serenaded her in front of a huge televised audience. Keith rarely talked about his patients as per his code of proper conduct, and frankly he was never as impressed or tongue-tied as I was. To him, all his patients were important. Their teeth were the stars.

I, on the other hand, thought I'd lose my mind with the prospect of meeting the goddess of music. Rhonda and I spent some of our happiest hours singing to the *Tapestry* album, her first big, splashy album. We would sit in our casement window facing Yellowstone Blvd., holding my cat, Strawberry, just like Carole's album cover, and belt out every song on that album.

Pedestrians passing by ignored these two raggedy girls while they sang "Beautiful" and "You've Got a Friend" almost as if we were starting an inspirational street choir. Carole resonated with us because she was a Jewish girl from one of the five boroughs with a head full of ethnic curls and a warmth that was obvious. If she could become a star, then maybe I could be a somebody too. Of course there was that small detail of tremendous talent necessary for this to happen, but I never liked to get bogged down by details.

I was going to meet this icon and how would she see me? A mom from Scarsdale? I wanted her to see me like I saw her, *a natural woman*. No easy feat for a woman who had done quite a bit of renovation to this fixer upper. If you ask me my actual hair color, I don't think I can remember. Meanwhile, Keith was shouting from the other room, "Let's get going! Get dressed. We gotta go!" You'd think he *was* an obstetrician at that moment and his patient was fully effaced.

I quickly sorted through my closet and found this beautiful, very old, peasant blouse and I knew it was perfect. I remember wearing almost the exact same blouse back in the late '80s at a Carole King concert in Central Park. I shook out my curls, threw on a pair of jeans and a leather jacket, and I was ready. I wasn't fooling anyone. I looked like an unkempt suburban housewife with an urge to be "the cool mom."

We got into our Mini Cooper, and I immediately tried to find a soft rock radio station. I decided it would be super cool if one of Carole's greatest hits started and we could "skat" along. Thankfully, my dreamboat dentist knew me all too well, so he found a Beatles Block, and that was his kind way of saying, "I'm doing this for your benefit." Got to love someone who knows how to protect you from your own stupidity.

We made our way into the city to pick her up on the Upper West Side at a friend's apartment. I was getting so nervous. I had fantasized all the way down the Henry Hudson Parkway how Carole and I were going to become best friends. *Maybe I'll invite her for a sleepover!* In other words, I was spiraling.

Finally, we pulled up to the building and there the queen was, standing outside waiting for us! Like a person. Someone you were picking up to go to Zabars for some smoked salmon.

I got out of the front passenger seat to greet Carole and (ok, let me just mention this was before we understood "my body my choice") I gave her a big sweaty hug. Gratefully, she hugged me back. I climbed into the back seat, right behind the goddess. I was so nervous that when Carole asked me a basic question, like "How are your kids doing?" I went into some kind of temporary stroke where words had disappeared, and I could practically smell almonds and toast. My answer, which I'm not proud of was "BEHHHUNIDDD." In other words, I became unintelligible.

Let me mention here that after a twenty-year career representing some of the most heralded and famous actors, I had never been this tongue-tied. And to give an example, James Earl Jones, the real Darth Vader, once yelled at me (for a good reason at the time), and that did not leave me this speechless.

I knew I needed to calm down, so I started to breathe. Being the genius that she was, I knew I wasn't the first super fan to lose her mind, but probably never in a tiny sedan with her dentist at the wheel. Carole calmed me by asking specific questions about our summer plans, and slowly I began to relax.

All through the ride down to Gramercy Park, I stared at Carole's famous curls. They were right in front of me, practically vibrating. I knew what I had to do before we arrived at the office. I was overwhelmed with an urge to touch her hair. I know, we all know, it's grossly inappropriate, I get it, but honestly how could I not? I didn't want to be obvious, just a real quick touch. Just a mild, curly tonsorial petting.

Mission accomplished without her even realizing I had got up in there for that brief but brilliant moment.

Unfortunately, there was little traffic to slow down this bacchanal and we arrived all too soon. I looked at my palms, assuming a stigmata would appear and deciding it might be a while before these hands got washed. Keith quickly took care of Carole, and we all walked back outside and said our goodbyes. Carole had a lunch date, and I was still in a fugue-like state when we got back into our car. I couldn't stop thinking about how Keith gifted me with this magical morning and how I wished my sister was alive so I could call her and recount every minute of this fantastical Sunday. I chose to believe she was with me in that Mini Cooper, probably giving me the courage to touch that greatness.

ACKNOWLEDGMENTS

THANK YOU TO KEITH, MY TROPHY HUSBAND, and to my entire family, Kira, Lindsey, and Ryan and their dad for putting up with my nonsense all these years by listening to these stories on repeat and for their generosity by allowing me to talk about them on stage and in this book.

To everyone who has given me massive amounts of material without prior permission. (Ooops! All with love and affection.)

Big thanks to David Crabb, my friend and mentor; Sara Barron for getting me to start writing; and Claudette Sutherland for her endless support and wise counsel. To Mark Gompertz for his patience and knowledge, and to Emily Flake for creating St. Nell's, which got my tush in the writing seat. A big thank you to every storytelling show for allowing me to share the stage and tell my stories, especially Kevin Allison, Erin Barker, Drew Prohaska, Susan Seliger, Georgia Clarke, and Generation Women. Special hip hip hooray to Frank Ruy for spending three years creating a lovely film about me with an enormous amount of patience and dedication.

Gratitude and the big trophy go to Azul Terronez, Steve Vannoy, and every genius at Authors Who Lead and Mandala Tree Press for being my cheerleader and making my words coherent.

Meet Sandi

SANDI MARX is a New York-based storyteller and comedian who has been touring the country for the past eight years. She has appeared on PBS's *Stories from the Stage* and can also be heard on dozens of podcasts, subjects ranging from dating to marriage/divorce, childrearing, and being a business woman. Sandi is the subject of an award-winning documentary titled *The Fabulist*.

After a mediocre career as an actress and a dancer, she became a talent agent and a partner at a prominent New York agency, Schiffman Ekman Morrison & Marx. After retiring from the agency business, she started writing and performing true stories about her adventures and mishaps.

Sandi is a mother of three grown kids and is a very overbearing grandma to a brilliant and beautiful toddler named Jack.

If you enjoyed this book,
please leave a review on Amazon.

Visit me at

SANDIJMARX.COM

where you can sign up for email updates and
follow along with my continuing adventures!

THANK You!

Printed in the USA
CPSIA information can be obtained
at www.ICGtesting.com
CBHW020305310124
3899CB00004B/19

9 781954 801776